All the B ...

Death by Incarceration

-A True Story

MJ Maccalupo

Write Beyond
Publishing

ISBN-13: 978-0-9964378-1-3

ISBN-10: 0-9964378-1-9

Published by *Write Beyond Publishing*, Wilmington, NC

Printed in the United States of America

Website: http://mjmaccalupo.com
Email: contact@mjmaccalupo.com

Acknowledgements

I would like to acknowledge several people without whom this work would not exist. First, and foremost, is, of course, Larry Nicholas Stromberg, whose **life, loves** and **murders** are the essence of this book.

During our many conversations, he demonstrated his deep remorse for all those whose lives he forever changed. His life is now dedicated to helping others through his *Redemption Theater Ministry*.

Family members and close friends also played a role in shaping this narrative, especially Diane Stromberg, his mother, with whom I have also been in regular contact.

I want to thank Diane's brother, Nick Mamallis, who first contacted me about writing this book.

Several of Stromberg's aunts & a niece shed new light on some areas of his life.

Stromberg's sister, Michelle, was also helpful in detailing a childhood of abuse that she and her brother endured.

His friends and fellow actors, filmmakers & videographer Larry Kirschner, Norman Macera and Sal DaRigo were also helpful in being able to see Stromberg from a different perspective, both as an actor and as a friend.

Also, Jack DiSarno, who not only accompanied me on the long trek to State Correctional Institution at Graterford, Pennsylvania to interview Stromberg, his family and friends, he also took on the task of helping with the editing of this book.

And, finally, my wife, Gigi, who meticulously went through these pages and made many suggestions for revision that helped to shape the final form of this book.

Dedication

This book is dedicated to the lost and tattered souls that they might find a way back to the grace of God, through Jesus Christ, his son, our Lord.

Death by Incarceration

Introduction
January 29, 2016

Death by Incarceration was neither written to advocate nor garner sympathy for Stromberg; but, rather to tell his story; what he has lived through and what he had done in his life — *the good, the bad and the horrific.*

*   *   *

On Friday, January 29, 2016, I received a voice message about a book project. It was from a man named Nick Mamallis, someone I had never spoken with or met. And from that call came this book — **Death by Incarceration.**

In his message, he mentioned a piece of writing that I might be interested in doing; the life of his nephew serving two consecutive life sentences for the stabbing deaths of his wife and mother-in-law. His nephew's name is, or was, Larry Stromberg; now known simply by: DG-6379.

At my first meeting with Mamallis, we talked over coffee at a fast-food restaurant in Leland, NC. It was there that he handed me an envelope containing 91 hand-written pages by and about the life of Larry Nicholas Stromberg, his nephew. Mamallis is brother to Diane Stromberg, Stromberg's mother.

Stromberg, whom I also had never met, spoken with or even heard of up until that day, was serving two consecutive life sentences at the State Correctional Institution at Graterford outside of Philadelphia, Pennsylvania for the stabbing deaths of his estranged wife, Stefan Stromberg, and her mother, Paula Rathgeb, on April 28, 1996.

What warrants the readers' attention is neither his childhood, nor the murders of the two women, which, at the risk of sounding callous (while a horrific crime) occurred over 20 years ago. Sadly, it seems that crimes as bad or worse happen almost daily now.

No, it was both the abuse Stromberg suffered and the murders he committed, coupled with what he has done since being in prison for the past 20 years. It is a story of **Abuse, Murder and Redemption**.

Stromberg first called on March 11, 2016. From that time forward our conversations have spanned many topics. We have corresponded via U.S. mail as well as email in addition to regular phone calls. Much of what has been written or spoken is included in his story, as well as our conversation during a visit to see him at S.C.I. Graterford in mid-July 2016.

His story is one that shows the all-to-real cycle of the life of an abused child surrounded by turmoil, who grows up to be an abuser and a murderer. Stromberg now finds hope and redemption through using his talent to daily demonstrate his faith in Jesus Christ.

2

This is a story about someone dedicated to winning the battle of **Spiritual Warfare** and helping others in their fight against the demons that control their lives. For some, those demons are simply free will, while others see them as otherworldly spirits that are attempting to disrupt their lives. Either way, we all have these demons. How we choose to deal with them is up to each of us.

The author is neither an attorney, nor involved in the legal process in any way; therefore, an apology is given here for any error in legal procedure or terminology, or for any technical errors as well.

One final note: The names of people who were neither directly involved in the trial nor who have been interviewed have been changed to protect their identity.

*   *   *

1

The Trial

May 21 – June 9, 1997

The killing is what the trial lays out, while the dying is what the family and friends experience.

Death by Incarceration was the verdict, or at least its meaning for Larry Nicholas Stromberg, who was soon to become inmate # DG-6379.

He sat motionless, staring ahead, his mind and body numb from a cocktail made up of Ativan, Sinequan and Risperdal that was now coursing through his veins. Unable to speak or comprehend what was happening to him, he knew he deserved to be there.

Stromberg was on trial for his life after taking the lives of two women who didn't deserve to die – especially in the brutal way that they did.

Watching as the world in that dank and ominous courtroom spun around him, he heard the words, sometimes registering, sometimes not, being thrown across the room to sway the jury one way or another. Yet, while he remained silent due in part to his lethargic state, his words, despite his not taking the stand, were used against him.

His only defense, since he confessed to the murders and his mother-in-law's dying last words naming him as the killer, was an insanity defense. And unlike any other defense, the defense counsel must show that the defendant was insane at the time of the crime. It is their burden, not the prosecutions.

The assistant district attorney, Carlos Vega, cleverly used an interview Stromberg did on May 7, 1996 (within a week of the murders) with a nationally syndicated television program (popular at that time) called *Hard Copy*. This decision to do the interview was made by his first defense lawyer, Vladimir Zdrok, who got paid by *Hard Copy* for having Stromberg tell his story and answer questions in the interview.

And the prosecution took full advantage of this opportunity by having a psychiatrist, John O'Brien, M.D., testify as one of their witnesses to rebut Julie B. Kessel's, M.D., the defense's psychiatrist, testimony as to Stromberg's sanity at the time just following the murders. Dr. O'Brien did this based on a brief examination of Stromberg and from watching that *Hard Copy* interview, (which he relied on heavily) which was shown to the jury as well. This carried a great deal of weight in refuting the defense's insanity plea. Oddly, neither psychiatrist examined Stromberg right after the murders and his surrender. It was only after the trial began a year later that either were hired to do this.

The case now being made against him by the prosecution, was edging ever closer to the result they were determined to get – the death penalty. All the while, the defense attorney was looking for a way to use the prosecutor's argument to his advantage in hopes to convince the jury that Stromberg was insane at the time of the murders.

The courtroom was packed with friends and family members of the defendant as well as those of the slain women, along with reporters and curious members of the community that had waited in line to win a space in the crowded room. Many sat through the almost 13 days of procedure, argument, testimony and evidence presented by both sides.

Stromberg sat silent, only half aware that he was in a fight for his life. His mind spinning from the drugs, tortured by the pain he caused, haunted by the ghosts of his rage.

Local and national newspapers and television news stations told the story of his crime for weeks after it occurred. Family members were 'rounded-up' for the big interview, the exposé, and the tell-all show that would win the best ratings — but at what price? Two murdered women, one mentally disturbed man, and many broken lives.

Newspaper articles all began with a description of Stromberg's acting career that had yet to take off, such as "City Actor Sought in Killing…", "'Crazy' Actor Sought…", "Ex-actor…", "Horror Movie-maker…", and on and on. But that is what he was, not who he was.

Regardless of the humanity, stories sell papers, and to compete for sales they must sensationalize an already horrific tragedy to titillate a hungry audience of readers. They pander to the drooling masses that live in a bubble of comfort and safety, many who long for such tragedies to read about, to watch on TV and to regurgitate with excited animation to friends and family as if they were actually at the apartment, witnessing the murders.

But they weren't; only Stromberg, his estranged wife, Stefan, and mother-in-law, Paula, were there; all wishing that they weren't.

While the prosecution offered up a picture of a man who was driven by abnormal jealousy and uncontrollable anger, the defense attempted to show a different portrait of the man. A man driven to wits end and beyond. A man driven over the edge because of his wife's alleged infidelity and abortion of what he believes to have been his own unborn child. A crazed killer who became a product of his own creation; the monstrous character named "Von Kraven" in his movie *Spiritual Warfare*. He became that vengeful character and did just what the character had done in the movie (at that time yet to be completed and released).

Stromberg, the actor, was also becoming a filmmaker as well. *Spiritual Warfare* was the second horror film that he wrote, directed and starred in.

The assistant D.A. went point-by-point detailing how Stromberg planned the murder(s) and executed his plan. The State wanted a first-degree murder conviction resulting in the death penalty. According to the District Attorney's account of the crime, Stromberg got up that morning with every intention of killing his wife. Dressed in dark clothing, he packed a backpack with knives and swords, traveled the 30 or so minutes by bus from where he was now residing to the apartment he and his wife once shared located in an old mansion in the area of Philadelphia known as Germantown.

Assistant D.A. Vega confidently explained to the judge and jury that Stromberg had all day to change his mind, but failed to do so. It was on the evening of April 28, 1996, that he made his move.

The prosecution pointed out that Stromberg went to the apartment believing he would catch Stefan with the lover he thought she was seeing, an Asian cook. The cook worked at *Long's Gourmet Chinese Restaurant* downtown where Stefan worked part-time. But, instead Stromberg found her with her mother, packing her belongings for a final trip to Florida and to safety with her mother and step-father.

Besides his confession, the police had other damaging evidence of his guilt. There was no question that he had committed this unimaginable crime.

The only arguable questions that remained were – was he sane when he murdered these two women and was it premeditated.

The prosecution described the murders as the premeditated murder of his wife and, the spontaneous murder of his mother-in-law. The assistant D.A. was voracious in his attack against Stromberg.

While the arena inside the rail made up of judge, jury, and lawyers, spun a web cloaked in the cold, hard language of law, the audience behind this barrier saw this as that of two humans' lives ending tragically, regardless of intent, motivation or passion.

If this were merely a story of a double homicide and the resulting conviction and sentencing (except for the details) it would end here. But it's not. 'The devil *is* in the details'. And in this case the devil played an even bigger role in this story.

Although Stromberg was assigned a public defender (Neil Jokelson), he didn't end up with one, even though he had little access to the kind of money it would take to hire an attorney of his own choosing. Fortunately, or unfortunately for him, because he was a trainer at the *Riverside Aquatic and Fitness Center* in Bala Cynwyd, PA, a very popular health club, he knew several of Philadelphia's prominent lawyers.

And, of course, with any high-profile case, high-dollar lawyers are readily available to represent the accused. A case like this, if it goes to trial (and it would), can boost the reputation of any lawyer – win or lose.

Shortly after Stromberg turned himself in at the police station downtown (called 'the roundhouse') a lawyer he knew, named Vladimir Zdrok, showed up and said that he would help him. Stromberg knew Zdrok from the *Riverside Fitness Club* where he had worked for seven years as a personal trainer. Zdrok came back a few days later when Stromberg had been transferred to the Philadelphia Detention Center with two contracts for Stromberg to sign and a film crew waiting at the door:

One was an agreement for representation in the criminal case for $100,000, plus costs. The other was an agreement for Zdrok to represent the defendant as an agent to negotiate all contracts and all income producing opportunities concerning the defendant's life story and all other matters for which Zdrok was to be compensated in the amount of 25% of all income which the defendant would earn.

On the same day that he had the defendant execute the two (2) agreements, Zdrok appeared at the prison with a film crew from the nationally televised show *Hard Copy* and instructed the defendant to submit to an interview. Zdrok was to be compensated for his role regarding the *Hard Copy* interview, but the defendant was to receive no compensation.[1]

The unfortunate consequence of subjecting Stromberg to this interview was that he "would be giving up his Fifth Amendment right to remain silent" at his trial – even if he never uttered a word in the witness stand. The tape was all that the prosecution needed for Stromberg to tell what happened; that, and Dr. O'Brien, who relied heavily on that tape to determine Stromberg's sanity at the time of the murders.

Within days after this interview Zdrok was replaced with another lawyer Stromberg knew from the fitness center. Zdrok was, in fact, the one who brought in Nino Tinari and his wife to speak with Stromberg. Tinari then became his trial attorney.

Over one year later, beginning on May 21, 1997, with Tinari as his attorney, Stromberg sat quietly in his disoriented state-of-mind as the trial moved ahead for over a two-week period. It ended on June 6, 1997 when a jury convicted Stromberg of "one count of first-degree murder, one count of second-degree murder, burglary, possessing an instrument of crime (PIC), and contempt for the violation of a court order."[2]

In Pennsylvania, as is true in many states, they have a bifurcated system; that is, there are two separate parts to the trial. First, there is the guilt phase, which establishes the innocence or guilt of the defendant. If he or she is found guilty, then the second phase kicks in; this is the penalty phase, which determines what the penalty for the crime(s) will be.

If the jury finds the defendant guilty, but cannot decide on the punishment in the second phase of the trial, the judge will determine what the penalty is to be – within stipulated guidelines, of course.

During the guilt phase of the trial, witnesses, one after the other, day after day, were called up to testify as to Stromberg's character or lack thereof. On one side, they were there to help the prosecution show premeditation and sanity. The assistant D.A. argued the murders were brought on by extreme jealousy and a relationship that was at best stormy and at worst destructive. For the defense, Tinari tried to show a life of abuse and mental illness that would demonstrate an insane state of mind at least in the time leading up to and at the time the murders took place.

While the trial began on Wednesday, May 21, 1997, the opening statements didn't commence until the following Wednesday, May 28 with Tinari relying on an insanity defense.

*　　　*　　　*

11

2

Witnesses for the Prosecution

On April 28, 1996, at approximately 7:30 p.m., defendant Larry Stromberg entered the apartment of his estranged wife, Stefan Stromberg, located at 251 West Walnut Lane in Philadelphia, and repeatedly stabbed her and her mother, Paula Rathgeb with a knife…When the police arrived, Mrs. Stromberg was unconscious, but Mrs. Rathgeb was able to disclose to police that the defendant was the attacker… Both women died as a result of their wounds…

Although the defendant and his wife had always had a 'stormy' relationship, their marriage began to deteriorate substantially in the summer and fall of 1995… Mrs. Stromberg, who had been working as a waitress at a restaurant owned by her friend, Pham Long, had an affair with a man who also worked at the restaurant… She became pregnant and traveled to Florida in January 1996 to stay with her mother and stepfather and to have an abortion… When Mrs. Stromberg returned from Florida, the couple tried to work out their differences… Defendant, an actor and personal trainer, saw a marriage counselor and also spoke constantly and obsessively to his friends and co-workers about his marital problems…[1]

In conversations with Stromberg he talked at length about his discussions with friends, neighbors, co-workers and clients alike about his situation with his wife. He was looking to anyone who could help him to provide the answer to make this nightmare go away. But, much like his childhood abuse, he couldn't find the right answer to help himself.

> In April 1996, about two weeks before the murders, defendant came to witness Mildred Lilly's apartment, which was in the same building as the Strombergs' apartment… He was upset and told Ms. Lilly that Mrs. Stromberg was saying that he had raped her… As a result of the alleged rape, on April 18, 1996, Mrs. Stromberg obtained a restraining order against defendant… During that period of time, Paula Rathgeb, Mrs. Stromberg's mother, became concerned about the situation and traveled from Florida to be with her daughter… Mrs. Stromberg and Mrs. Rathgeb stayed at a Best Western hotel under the assumed name of 'Cohen.'[2]

Stefan, as did her mother, knew that Stromberg could be pushed to violence. So, they tried to hide from him in order to make their safe journey back to Florida.

"On April 26, 1996, Mr. Stromberg obtained a final protection from abuse order which was to remain in effect until April 26, 1997…"[3]

The prosecution began testimony by calling up, the first two officers to arrive on the scene. The first, Officer Trenwith of the Mobile Crime Detection Unit, testified that:

"…he arrived at the crime scene, 251 West Walnut Lane, Philadelphia, Pennsylvania, ground floor apartment, at approximately 10:45 p.m., and proceed to photograph the scene, collect evidence, take measurements, prepare sketches and collect blood samples."[4]

Next, police officer Kaluza testified that on April 28, 1996, he entered the rear of the building at 251 West Walnut Lane and found Stefan Stromberg and Paula Rathgeb both lying on the floor in pools of heavy dark blood. He stated that Stefan was alive, but unable to speak and that Paula was on her back with one foot on a chair. She had cuts on her face, hands and arms. Kaluza testified that Rathgeb, when asked who did this, responded, "Larry Stromberg."[5]

According to Stromberg and the eyewitness testimony, the murders took place at approximately 7:30 p.m. that Sunday, April 28, 1996. Officer Trenwith arrived over three hours later to photograph the crime scene, while Officer Kaluza arrived, shortly after the murders, responding to the call made by Mildred Lilly.

Next, to testify was Mildred Lilly, a neighbor at the same West Walnut address. She had been a friend to both Stefan and Stromberg alike.

She testified for the prosecution that she was aware of the marital problems that the Strombergs were experiencing. She also stated that she was aware that sometime in late December 1995 or early January 1996, Stefan had driven to Florida to have an abortion brought about by her affair with a co-worker at the Chinese restaurant where she worked part-time. She learned this from both Stefan and Stromberg in conversations that she had with each of them.

Lilly testified that she was aware that Stefan had obtained a restraining order against Stromberg in mid-April. Lilly also testified that she was told by Stefan that she was raped by Stromberg, thus causing Stefan to take out the restraining order. This was objected to as hearsay, and the Court sustained this objection, but in later testimony Lilly testified that "I believe that he (defendant) had raped Stefan." This was allowed, over objection by the defense counsel.

Lilly also testified that she had been helping Stefan and Paula (Stefan's mother) pack for Stefan's move to Florida. This was on April 28, 1996, shortly before Stromberg burst in to commit the murders. Lilly was returning home when she saw Stromberg run toward the apartment saying, "Now is the time. Now is the time."

She stated that she heard the screams of Paula Rathgeb and Stefan Stromberg and then she called 911.[6]

Ms. Lilly had a sympathetic ear that both Stromberg and Stefan felt they could confide in with their deepest most emotions and personal matters. She became one of the star witnesses for the prosecution.

Ms. Pham Long was a second important witness for the prosecution in this trial. She was the owner of a family Chinese gourmet restaurant in the downtown Philadelphia area. She employed Stefan as a part-time waitress and hostess there. And that is where Stefan met the cook that she began an affair with, eventually becoming pregnant. She told Stromberg that the baby was his, but had also told him that it was the cook's baby. The newspaper reports speculated that it was Stromberg's. To this day, Stromberg believes that it was his.

While Long knew Stromberg, she had a strong bond with his wife, Stefan, and no real loyalty to him.

Long testified that she owned the restaurant where Stefan and the cook both worked. She also testified that she knew of the extra-marital affair that Stefan was having with this cook at Christmas time in 1995.

Long also testified that she knew that Stefan went to Florida to have an abortion after becoming pregnant by the cook. She further stated that she knew that upon Stefan's return, she and Stromberg went to counseling to try to save their marriage.

Further in her testimony, Long stated that Stefan told her that Stromberg had raped and strangled her. In a final statement Long told the Court that she was supposed to meet both Stefan and Paula on Sunday, April 28, 1996, but learned of their murders prior to her leaving to meet up with them.

Long's statement regarding the rape and strangulation was objected to and a motion for a mistrial was requested, since hearsay evidence is generally not admissible. This, however, was allowed by Judge Glazer. [7]

Following these two important witnesses were several others that testified to various aspects that led up to and included the murders.

An attorney that Stefan Stromberg had hired to obtain a 'protection from abuse' order also testified.

16

Margaret Klaw testified that she was an attorney retained by Stefan on April 24, regarding a protection from abuse order that she had sought. Klaw testified that on April 26, Stromberg agreed in court to stay away from Stefan for one year, until April 26, 1997.[8]

Another neighbor, Candice Adicair, then testified that she had been present helping Stefan and Paula pack on that fateful night. She also testified that she had heard Stromberg make disparaging remarks about Stefan being overweight.[9]

In conversations with Stromberg he talked about the protection order and the details of what went on between them during this time.

He verified that a protection order was in place, but that Stefan was the one who initiated their meeting, thus violating the order. Stromberg also stated that Stefan told him that she would have it removed and that she wanted them to "work things out" and be a couple again, just like it had been in the beginning of their relationship.

He was still so much in love with her, and controlled by her, that he willingly violated the order and met with her.

In writing and conversation, he repeatedly referred to the two times he and Stefan were together just before the murders; and that he had forced himself on her. He adds that after he began forcing himself on her she allowed, and even participated in, the sexual contact. Stromberg, however, understands that this is still rape.

In addition to Ms. Lilly's eyewitness testimony concerning seeing Stromberg run into the house dressed in black, a second eyewitness took the stand to corroborate Ms. Lilly's testimony.

> Lisa Zollinger testified that on April 28, 1996, she was visiting her boyfriend at 229 West Walnut Lane at about 7:30 p.m. or 8:00 p.m., when in the back yard of the house next door, she saw a white male, dressed in black, crouching low with a knapsack over his shoulder running into a house. She then heard screaming and saw the person come running out of the house with the knapsack. [10]

While the murder weapon was never found, Stromberg's knapsack was found by Nicholas Teti, a contractor who was rehabilitating a house in the area. He discovered it under a pile of tires and trash. Oddly enough, while Teti found the knapsack with all the items Stromberg had place there, he did not, nor did investigators afterward, ever recover the knife that Stromberg used to kill Stefan and Paula. [11]

In a recent telephone conversation with Stromberg, when asked of the whereabouts of the murder weapon he replied that, to the best of his recollection, he had thrown it into the same dumpster where he had disposed of the knapsack. He contends that, at that time, he was in a frenzied, confused state and had just thrown these objects into the dumpster as he ran through one of the alleyways after leaving the apartment.

The knife, he said, was a large folding knife that his father had given him in 1980, as a gift.

As Stromberg's words corroborate, the contents of the canvas bag were: "two large knives, a hammer, a nightstick, a prayer book, a ski mask, and a note pad with notations indicating that it had been presented to Stefan Stromberg."[12]

The next to testify was Police Officer Clyde Jones. He was the officer that served the Protection from Abuse order to Stromberg that was obtained by Stefan Stromberg and Paula Rathgeb.

"He testified that the defendant told him, when he was leaving, that his wife would regret this when he made it big."[13]

Ernest Neill Rathgeb, Paula Rathgeb's husband, testified that Stefan had come to Florida in late 1995 and early 1996, where he and Paula resided, to visit them and have an abortion.[14]

Several other officers testified as to what they found at the crime scene at various points in the investigation. One Detective, Leon Lubiejewski, of the Homicide Division, testified that he was at the scene on April 31, 1996, "to process the crime scene, collect evidence and supervise the sketching of the premises. He searched the area to find a murder weapon, but was unsuccessful."[15]

Another officer, Sergeant Ernie Oakley, was directed to secure the scene outside. He spoke to people in the area to locate potential witnesses and spoke with Mildred Lilly. He discovered that she had an answering machine tape with a message on it that could be used as evidence; he confiscated the tape.

He also spoke with Mr. Augustus Montgomery, the owner of the property being renovated, who surrendered the black canvas bag containing the items, previously mentioned, to the police. He was Mr. Teti's employer, the workman who found the bag containing the items belonging to Stromberg. Teti had turned them over to Montgomery.[16]

As the days of the trial moved on, other members of law enforcement, who were assigned to this case, were put on the stand by the prosecution to present details of the investigation to the jury.

> Detective William Egenlauf...testified that on May 1, 1996, he obtained and executed a search warrant for Mr. Stromberg's residence at #7 Elmwood Drive, Lower Merion, Pennsylvania, and confiscated a knapsack and certain books...At a sidebar conference, it was revealed that the books and magazines recovered concerned horror films, mass murder and serial killers. The Court sustained the trial counsel's objection to the subject matter of these books being made known to the jury at this time and ruled that they may be relevant for rebuttal only. [17]

The next detective to testify presented some very important information to the jury about Stromberg after his surrender on May 1, 1996.

> William Danks, a retired homicide detective, testified that on April 28, 1996, he went to the crime scene to look for evidence and found some knives...He further testified that on May 1, 1996, he obtained an arrest warrant for the defendant and his attempts to serve the warrant in Lower Merion were unsuccessful...He further testified that on May 1, 1996, while working at Homicide at about 11:30

p.m., Mr. Stromberg surrendered with another man (Neil Abrams) and gave Detective Danks a bag and said "these are the clothes I was wearing the night I killed my wife and my mother-in-law"... Detective Danks then took the defendant into custody, testified that he warned him of his constitutional rights and took a statement in which the defendant admitted losing control of himself because his wife, Stefan, was cheating on him, going to her apartment with a knife and hitting Stefan and her mother with the knife... Detective Danks testified that during the statement, defendant was alert, responsive, coherent and responded to his questions appropriately. [18]

The final witness testimony presented by the prosecution was given by Dr. Carolyn Revercomb, the Assistant Medical Examiner who:

> ...testified that the cause of both deaths was multiple stab wounds and the manner of deaths was homicide.
>
> The defendant stipulated that the clothing handed to Detective Danks by the defendant had human blood on the pants of Type B the same as both victims' blood. The Commonwealth then rested its case.
>
> The Court denied a defense Motion for Judgment of Acquittal. [19]

One of the points of contention as to the medical examiner's testimony was the editorializing that she did while responding to the prosecutor's questions.

Dr. Revercomb engaged in the following dialog:

COMMONWEALTH: With respect to Paula Rathgeb and the type of injury she has to her back, are those

21

patterned very much life Stefan's or are they different?

WITNESS: There are some differences. However, when I performed these two examinations, I was struck by the similarity of the injuries. **It's as though someone really intended for these people to die**. *[emphasis added]*

DEFENSE COUNSEL: Objection and move to strike, Your Honor. Move for a mistrial.

THE COURT: Motion to strike granted. Motion for mistrial denied.

DEFENSE COUNSEL: May we have a cautionary instruction to the jury?

THE COURT: Yes. Members of the jury, would you disregard that last comment, please.[20]

But, as we all know, the damage was done.

All the while, Stromberg sat in silence, half aware that his fate was about to be decided by 12 strangers. The death penalty was what the prosecution was working toward as its goal. The defense, because of overwhelming evidence, testimony and Stromberg's own confession, had few tools in their bag with which to work. Not Guilty by Reason of Insanity (NGRI), was Tinari's best defense.

After all, he did snap, he was hearing voices, seeing shadows moving around him, was pushed farther than he was capable of going with infidelity, abortion, reconciliation and rejection, and a lifetime of physical, sexual and emotional abuse.

He sat there living in a lifeless shell, doped up and without love or hope anywhere to be found. Stromberg was as low as one can get, suicidal and lost.

How does one help a person who can't or won't help himself? That was the task at hand for Tinari.

*　　　*　　　*

3

Witnesses for the Defense

Nino Tinari, Stromberg's attorney began his defense by attempting to prove that Stromberg was insane at the time of the murders.

While there are several, different standards used to determine a defendant's sanity in a trial in the United States, Pennsylvania uses the "M'Naghten Rule." This standard is applied to determine if a person meets the criteria established for a verdict of 'Not Guilty by Reason of Insanity' (NGRI).

*   *   *

In a telephone conversation on April 18, 2016, with Bryan Cohen, who was Stromberg's counseling psychologist, he was reticent to discuss Stromberg or his role as a witness in the court proceedings. When this contact was first initiated there was a long silence, after which he apologized and said that the call caught him by complete surprise.

After a brief introduction and general conversation, his insight was requested in order to better understand this case. Stromberg had given his name, and that of his mother, Dr. Sandra Cohen, who had treated both Stromberg and Stefan as well.

Cohen, after only a few minutes of courteous discussion, had a dramatic change in tone. His voice tightened and his words became more guarded. After a pause, he stated that he didn't wish to discuss his testimony at the trial. He then commented that this phone call brought back memories of the nightmares that he experienced after the time of the murders and his association with Stromberg and Stefan.

Tinari called Cohen to the stand first.

The first defense witness was Brian [*sic*] Cohen, a counseling psychologist who had counseled both defendant, Larry Stromberg and Stefan Stromberg, concerning their marital problems. Mr. Cohen testified that he diagnosed the defendant, Larry Stromberg, with adjustment disorder; mixed disturbance of conduct and emotion; intermittent explosive disorder; and partner relationship problems. This was as a result of his counseling of the defendant in 1996 for marital problems. Mr. Cohen testified concerning the defendant's increased anger over Stefan Stromberg's extra-marital affair and her abortion in Florida... He testified as to several joint sessions with both the defendant and Stefan Stromberg [in] which Mr. Stromberg displayed increasing rage... Mr. Cohen testified that he was concerned and referred Mr. Stromberg for psychiatric evaluation so that he could receive medication... Mr. Cohen testified that at a session with defendant on April 27, 1996, the defendant admitted that he had forced himself upon his wife sexually.[1]

Next came a series of character witnesses, associates from the fitness center and from his acting jobs; all supporting the assertion that Stromberg was a good employee, trainer, actor, etc. until his wife, Stefan, had the affair and abortion.

They attested to his change in demeanor and working ability; that it was much diminished due to his new obsession with his marriage and its problems. They all were privy to his marital problems through his discussion with them and/or their observations of him and, in some cases, his wife, Stefan.

One of the character witnesses, Russell Axelrod, who was an associate of Stromberg's from the fitness center, also represented him in Family Court regarding the protection from abuse order where Stromberg agreed to stay away from Stefan for one year, without admission of wrongdoing. "He testified that the defendant seemed 'out of it at that time'."[2]

An interesting comment made by one of the witnesses, a friend and filmmaking associate of Stromberg's, adds an almost eerie footnote to this horrific crime.

> Vincent C. Ellis testified that he was a filmmaker who knew the defendant since about June of 1995 as an actor when they met during the shooting of a horror film project of Mr. Stromberg. He later became his partner and his friend…
>
> Mr. Ellis testified that during the defendant's *Horrorscope* film project, which was financed by Neil Abrams, the defendant deteriorated because of his

problems… He testified that defendant sometimes would feel like the Von Kraven character in the *Horrorscope* movie.[3]

Von Kraven and his son, Eddie Kraven, are two evil characters in Stromberg's movie, *Horrorscope*. In the story the son, Eddie, takes over his father's killing rampage by going after those who murdered Von Kraven, his father.

In one part of the movie Von Kraven strangles and stabs a woman in a fit of rage, much like Stromberg had strangled and raped Stefan, and then later stabbed her and her mother.

After viewing the film, there seemed to be some similarities between the two, with the exception that Stefan and Paula's murders were not just a plot point in a horror film. These were two very alive women who suffered gravely during that awful night in April 1996.

Another associate from the fitness center testified that he was aware of the defendant's marital problems from their conversations and he also noticed a distinct deterioration in his affect. He wanted to help so he allowed Stromberg to move into his brother's duplex on Elmwood Avenue in Bala Cynwyd, just a few miles from the apartment on West Walnut Lane.

A friend from the fitness center who testified next was a man who was much more involved in Stromberg's life at the time than some of the others. He was a friend from the fitness center who, according to Stromberg, was dating his sister, Michelle, then.

Neil Abrams testified that he also knew the defendant from the Riverside gym for about eight (8) or nine (9) years and that he was also familiar with Stefan Stromberg and the marital problems with the couple. Neil Abrams testified that on the Tuesday following the incident, the defendant called him on the telephone seeking advice on how to surrender to the police in this matter... He met Larry Stromberg later that evening and took him to his home and sought advice from an FBI agent who was a friend of Mr. Abrams on how to surrender Mr. Stromberg... Mr. Abrams testified that he accompanied Mr. Stromberg to the roundhouse to surrender himself... He testified that during this period Mr. Stromberg was "rambling" and speaking as if his wife was still alive.[4]

Local newspapers, tabloids, television and radio stations were reporting the news of the murders, the surrender, and the arraignment. One station that dug into the story was WPVI-TV Channel 6 Action News, an ABC affiliate in Philadelphia.

This was a time when the news of the day was the Oklahoma City Bombing, which had occurred just one year prior to this crime, with Timothy McVeigh's trial set to begin just one month before Stromberg's in 1997; the infamous OJ Simpson trial, which was still in the news; the murder and dismemberment in Sparta, Michigan committed by Federico Luis Cruz on April 25, 1996, just three days before Stromberg's murders; and the auctioning off of Jeffrey Dahmer's refrigerator used to store the genitals of his male victims, his hatchet and other tools, all for one million dollars.

These stories were reported along with the murders of Stefan Stromberg and Paula Rathgeb, while the police were trying to locate the whereabouts of Larry Stromberg, the suspected killer.

After Stromberg's surrender, WPVI Action News broadcast an interview with Neil Abrams, one of Stromberg's friends. In the interview in early May 1996, Abrams related the phone conversation he had with Stromberg prior to his picking him up at Miles Park.

According to the report Stromberg called Abrams for help in how to go about surrendering to the police. The conversation went like this:

> Stromberg: "Lawyer, lawyer. . .What did I do? What did I do? Did I hurt anyone?"
> Friend: "Yes, you did."
> Stromberg: "Who?"
> Friend: "Your wife and your mother-in-law."
> Stromberg: "Oh, my God! Oh, my God! I don't believe it."

Stromberg then asked Abrams to give him instructions as to how to turn himself in. He told Stromberg he would pick him up to help him do that.

In the report, the friend (Abrams) picked Stromberg up at Miles Park in White Marsh township on the Germantown Pike. He was quoted as saying that when he (Abrams) arrived he found Stromberg lying on the ground, dirty and unshaven rambling incoherently as he rolled around. One of the news reports indicated that the murder weapon had not been found; this was later stated at the trial as well.

In a later taped television interview, just a week before the trial was scheduled to begin Tinari, Stromberg's attorney, went on record about the case. He was asked by the local television news interviewer why there hasn't been much media coverage of the case since last year. Tinari said that they had waited for things to die down about the case, because too much interest by the public for too long could cause a kind of fatigue or lack of any sympathy for the situation. He wanted the jury to hear the facts about the crime and that the accused, Larry Stromberg, was a person; a human who made a tragic mistake. Tinari was cautious to not divulge his defense strategy in the interview as the interviewer pressed him whether he would use the insanity defense or not.

Shortly after the trial began, Tinari hired a psychiatrist, Dr. Julie B. Kessel, to examine Stromberg.

At the trial, Dr. Kessel presented her findings as Tinari's evidence that Stromberg was insane at the time of the murders. This, his only viable defense; that of Not Guilty by Reason of Insanity (NGRI).

> Julie B. Kessel, M.D., Psychiatrist, testified as defense expert concerning the insanity issue. Dr. Kessel testified that she conducted a psychiatric evaluation of the defendant, gathered background information on the defendant in this case and came to the conclusion that the defendant suffered from a schizo-defective disorder, bi-polar type, which consist of two separate problems i.e., schizophrenia and depressive-manic conditions... She explained that his psychosis (loss of touch with reality) deteriorated over a period of time and with the deterioration, periods of hallucinations and delusions become more frequent... She testified that in 1988, Mr. Stromberg began to hear the voices of a character from one of his films, Von Kraven, and also heard the voice of God. It was her opinion that his psychosis started at this time... She testified that the defendant was actively

psychotic at the time of the incident and that he was not aware of what he was doing and did not know what he was doing was wrong.[5]

The Commonwealth informed the Court that it planned to call John O'Brien, M.D., a psychiatrist, as its rebuttal expert. The Commonwealth also informed the Court that Dr. O'Brien planned to play for the jury the videotape of the defendant's *Hard Copy* interview which was taken in prison on May 7, 1996. The Commonwealth informed the Court that Dr. O'Brien relied upon this videotape informing his rebuttal expert opinion... During the interchange concerning the *Hard Copy* tape, the record is clear that on May 7, 1996, when the defendant was interviewed, he was in the psychiatric ward of the prison on 'suicide observation'... He was prescribed anti-depressant medication... Furthermore, the Court observed, after viewing the tape, that the tape was admissible because the tape contained clear, unequivocal admissions of the defendant and shows his demeanor, appearance and behavior at a point and time relatively close to the event and that it was relied upon by the Commonwealth's expert.

John O'Brien, M.D., testified as rebuttal psychiatric expert for the Commonwealth. Dr. O'Brien testified that he conducted an evaluation of Mr. Stromberg by reviewing a number of different items and reference including the autopsy reports, the Mobile Crime Detection report, the search warrants, the arrest warrants, statements of witnesses, biographical information of the defendant and statement of the defendant... He testified that he used the *Hard Copy* videotape and interviewed the defendant at which time the *Hard Copy* videotape was played for the jury... Based upon all these factors, Dr. O'Brien's opinion

31

was that the defendant was not actively psychotic (out of touch with reality), but merely suffered from minor anxiety and depression not rising to a significant diagnostic level… Dr. O'Brien ultimately opined that the defendant at the time of the incident knew what he was doing and that it was wrong…

Dr. O'Brien testified that in reaching his opinion, he heavily relied on the *Hard Copy* tape and that it was a 'very important piece of information'.[6]

The defendant offered Dr. Kessel in its rebuttal case. Dr. Kessel disagreed with Dr. O'Brien's conclusions, and reaffirmed her opinion concerning the defendant's insanity and active psychosis.[7]

The defense then rested in rebuttal and the Commonwealth offered no sur-rebuttal.

During closing arguments, the prosecutor made reference to the defendant 'draped with an American flag'… the prosecutor defined first degree murder as 'cold blooded'… the prosecutor repeatedly made reference to the rape by the defendant of the victim Stefan Stromberg… the prosecutor told the jury that they could tell the defendant was not insane because he did not slap his lawyer during the course of the trial… the prosecutor commented on the untimeliness or lateness of the hiring of the defense expert to raise the insanity issue in this case… and the prosecutor referred to the defendant as 'an evil person' and as a 'bad person'.[8]

The prosecuting attorney appears to have invented a "slap your lawyer" test for rebutting an insanity plea.

There are several critical pieces that have thus far been left out; things that were integral to this case. First, and foremost, Assistant DA Vega, made an offer to Stromberg's attorney of third degree murder, which would have imposed a sentence of 40-80 years. Tinari confirms this in a written response (dated November 20, 2008) to Stromberg's letter asking if a plea bargain was offered and what were the terms.

A second thing of note in the prosecution's case was how the prosecutor used, as his expert rebuttal witness, Dr. O'Brien, a psychiatrist, who interviewed Stromberg only briefly and only after the trial was underway. He also did not interview the counselors that saw Stromberg and his wife, or Stromberg's family members (most importantly his mother).

As the trial document notes, Dr. O'Brien's opinion weighed heavily on the *Hard Copy* taped interview that was done on May 7, 1996, a week after the murders, and when Stromberg was heavily medicated and on suicide watch at the prison where he was being held pending the outcome of the trial.

Not having been there it is hard to understand if (or, maybe more precisely, why) the jury gave more weight to Dr. O'Brien's testimony than it did to Dr. Kessel's, given they both were equally qualified to diagnose Stromberg; with Kessel having the advantage of having spent more time with Stromberg evaluating his state of mind.

There were additional concerns that arise from this trial. While some off-handed remarks stated during the trial might seem over the top, the court allowed the attorneys to get away with them ("naked, draped with an American Flag", "cold blooded", "an evil person" and "a bad person").

Of course, even laymen know that attorneys will sometimes become quite flamboyant in their presentations to make a dramatic point. However, at no point was Stromberg ever "naked" or "draped with an American Flag".

The defense attorney, for his part, tried painting a picture of Stromberg as a man with the body of "an Adonis" and a mind of a child who still played with dolls from his youth, destroyed by abuse all his life. Again, courtroom drama.

Maybe both sides engaged in theatrics, but Stromberg, just like everyone else, is made up of many parts. In his case, some of those parts were created by the evil in this world, while others by the innocence of childhood – and still others came from within Larry Stromberg.

A guilty verdict was returned by the jury on June 6, 1997. On June 9, 1997, the penalty phase part of the trial was held at which time the jury failed to reach a verdict. The Court then imposed the sentence in this case.

Stromberg was sentenced by Judge Gary Glazer to two consecutive terms of life without parole for the first and second-degree murder convictions and an aggregate consecutive term of one hundred twenty (120) to two hundred forty (240) months incarceration on the remaining charges.[9]

Through the trial, the appeal and the failed appeals, Stromberg has had a steady stream of attorneys flowing in and out of his life. From Vladimir Zdrok, an acquaintance of Stromberg's from the fitness center, who represented him for only a week or so, to Nino Tinari (also from the fitness center), who represented Stromberg at the trial, and others, such as Neil Jokelson (a court appointed attorney).

34

Then there was Stromberg's attorney who presented his appeal to the Superior Court of Pennsylvania, which upheld the lower court's ruling.

Next, Daniel Rendine, who represented Stromberg, prepared an appeal petition to the Pennsylvania Supreme Court, which was denied.

After the Pennsylvania Supreme Court's denial of his appeal, Stromberg submitted a Post-Conviction Relief Act petition (PCRA). Unfortunately, he submitted it to the wrong court and had to resubmit. Subsequent to this, one of his previous lawyers reappeared – Neil Jokelson.

Jokelson was hired by Stromberg's family to represent him in Federal Court (Eastern District), but sat on the paperwork, never filing, until Stromberg was time-barred from presenting his appeal.

*   *   *

4
Media Hype
May 1996 – June 1997

As soon as the local press found out about the murders they were in full swing getting the story. They knew the names of the victims and soon learned that Paula's last words were to name Larry Stromberg, her son-in-law, as the murderer.

Once the media did some checking on Stromberg they found that he was an up-and-coming actor, a local celebrity of sorts. So, they headlined each article, whether in the tabloids or the 'legitimate' press with one catchphrase or another that led with either 'actor' or 'horror film' or something to do with his profession. Below are several such headlines and opening lines, but by no means a complete list.

The samples here represent coverage immediately after the murders (continuing for a week or so) and as the trial began one year later.

From *The Philadelphia Inquirer* **&** *The Daily News*:

MOTHER, DAUGHTER STABBED TO DEATH IN GERMANTOWN

by Suzette Parmley, *Inquirer* Staff Writer
Date: April 29, 1996
Publication: Philadelphia Inquirer, The (PA)

A Florida woman's visit to her daughter in Germantown ended tragically yesterday, with both of them stabbed to death and the daughter's husband sought in the slayings, police said...

Some reported just the facts, as in the one above which appeared the morning after the murders, while others (below) interviewed eye witnesses on the scene at the time of the murders as well as family members and friends. This one is from day two after the murders when more details and facts were uncovered.

*   *   *

CITY ACTOR SOUGHT IN KILLING OF WIFE AND MOTHER-IN-LAW...

by Lea Sitton and Thomas J. Gibbons Jr., *Inquirer* Staff Writers
Date: April 30, 1996
Publication: Philadelphia Inquirer, The (PA) Page: A01

Police yesterday searched for a struggling young actor whose wife and mother-in-law were stabbed to death in Germantown apartment on Sunday, 11 days after the wife sought court protection from him.

An arrest warrant issued early yesterday charged Larry Stromberg, 30, with two counts of murder and related offenses in the stabbings of Stefan Stromberg, 30, and Paula Rathgeb, 48, of Fort Lauderdale, Fla.

Friends and co-workers described Stromberg, one of the thousands of unknown Philadelphia performers looking for that big break, as intense and emotional. He had a penchant for producing independent horror films and was involved in *Rats in the Maze, Blades* and *Horrorscope...*

'He was never in any kind of trouble up until he met her,' Lawrence Stromberg said of his son...

The article goes into great detail about the events of the murder and the character of the murderer.

*   *   *

Others write the details of the crime with a sense of drama and a literary flair, as in some of the following articles.

BLADE RUNNER: TYPE-CAST AS A KILLER?...

by Jim Nolan, Don Russell and Joe O'Dowd, *Daily News* Staff Writers. Movie critic Gary Thompson contributed to this report.
Date: April 30, 1996
Publication: Philadelphia Daily News (PA) Page: 03

He steals with animal swiftness across the overgrown garden path to the back door of the darkened mansion, where a lone light illuminates his unsuspecting victims.

Neighbors' dogs start to bark. Moments later, the knife-wielding killer bursts through the door and carves his fury in blood – brutally stabbing the daughter in the face before turning the blade on her screaming mother.

It was like a scene from the kind of horror movies Larry Stromberg liked to make.

But this time...

*   *   *

FILMMAKER A FLOP IN ROLE OF HUBBY?...

by William Bunch and Marisol Bello, *Daily News* Staff Writers. Staff writers Gloria Campisi and Joe O'Dowd contributed to this report
Date: May 1, 1996
Publication: *Philadelphia Daily News* (PA) Page: 06

Larry Stromberg, the aspiring actor wanted in the knife murders of his wife and mother-in-law, could never win an Academy Award for the role of husband.

Even as a newlywed, Stromberg ignored his bride, Stefan. He went off to lift weights and shoot his low-budget horror flicks while hounding Stefan for her weekly paycheck, according to a neighbor who's a close friend of the couple.

It almost became a media circus – no, it did become one. Each writer trying to outdo the next by spinning the story in their own most enticing way.

*　　*　　*

HELLO LARRY: TOUGH GUY CALLED 'WIMP'...

by Marisol Bello and Jack McGuire, *Daily News* Staff Writers. Staff writers Gloria Campisi, Joe O'Dowd and Nicole Weisensee contributed to this report
Date: May 2, 1996
Publication: *Philadelphia Daily News* (PA) Page: 03

Horror flick tough guy Larry Stromberg tearfully confessed to the slashing murders of his estranged wife and her mother, police said yesterday.

Detectives said the hulking weight-lifter and aspiring actor became the 'ultimate wimp,' his massive body quivering, as he described the slayings...

Four days after the murders, reporters were grasping for new angles to tell the story. Stromberg the 'gentle monster' portrayed here, searching for the right metaphor, the best opposites, the yin and the yang; but what really was lacking in the descriptions was the possibility of a mentally ill man, driven beyond his ability to cope with life.

*　　*　　*

ACTOR SOUGHT IN STABBINGS GIVES UP POLICE SAY HE CONFESSED TO KILLINGS

by Jeff Gammage, *Inquirer* Staff Writer
Date: May 2, 1996
Publication: *Philadelphia Inquirer, The* (PA) Page: B01

A struggling young actor accused of killing his wife and mother-in-law in Germantown on Sunday has surrendered and confessed to the crimes, a senior Philadelphia police investigator said yesterday.

'He said he was upset, he did it, and he's sorry,' said the investigator, who spoke on the condition of anonymity...

*   *   *

ACTOR TOLD POLICE OF RAGE ON NIGHT OF DOUBLE SLAYING...

by Linda Loyd, *Inquirer* Staff Writer
Date: May 9, 1996
Publication: *Philadelphia Inquirer, The* (PA) Page: B01

Actor Larry Stromberg told police that he had flown into a jealous rage when he slashed his estranged wife and her mother a total of 34 times because he suspected his spouse was cheating on him...

Coverage died off after this, until a year later when the trial began (below).

*   *   *

LAWYER: ACTOR 'SNAPPED'

by Dave Racher, *Daily News* Staff Writer
Date: May 29, 1997
Publication: *Philadelphia Daily News* (PA) Page: 12

41

After his wife admitted cheating on him last year, actor Larry Stromberg transformed himself into the monster he played in a horror film, his lawyer told a jury yesterday.

Attorney Nino V. Tinari said the jealous Stromberg, 31, had been suffering from "psychotic episodes" that included 'talking to ghosts'...

*   *   *

Once both the guilt and sentencing phases had concluded the headlines rang out with the verdict and disposition of the case. Pre-trial they had depicted Stromberg as an aspiring actor whose "career has yet to take off," but now he became a "Bad Actor," "B-Movie Actor" and the like.

BAD ACTOR, REAL-LIFE KILLER/JURY NIXED INSANITY DEFENSE ...

by Dave Racher, *Daily News* Staff Writer
Date: June 7, 1997
Publication: *Philadelphia Daily News* (PA) Page 08

The B-movie actor's real-life role as an insane, jealous killer did not make it past the cutting-room floor...

*   *   *

ACTOR CONVICTED IN SLAYINGS OF WIFE AND HER MOTHER...

by Linda Loyd, *Inquirer* Staff Writer
Date June 7, 1997
Publication: *Philadelphia Inquirer, The* (PA) Page B01

B-movie actor Larry Stromberg was convicted yesterday of the slashing of his estranged wife and her mother after he learned that his wife was leaving him…

*   *   *

TWO LIFE TERMS FOR FILM ACTOR…

by Dave Racher, *Daily News* Staff Writer
Date: June 10, 1997
Publication: *Philadelphia Daily News* (PA) Page: 18

It was the final curtain for the B-movie actor, and he spoke on cue.

'I'm not some evil monster,' said Larry Stromberg as he was about to be sentenced to two consecutive life-prison terms for killing his wife and mother-in-law…

*   *   *

Other news organizations in print and online wrote about this murder and trial. Some analyzing the main people, Stromberg and Stefan, developing opinions based on what information they could glean from friends and neighbors, while others reporting only what they knew at the time in as factual a manner as they could.

An article by Gerald McOscar, Esq. in the August 1997 issue of "The Liberator" entitled, "Slap Your Spouse – Lose Your House" discusses some of the aspects of the Stromberg case. That is, 'Does taking out a protection-from-abuse order incite a spouse to use violence'. In this case, he makes a very important point. The point he makes refers to a note that Stromberg received; one that Stefan wrote to Stromberg after she had the protection-from-abuse order served. More specifically, this was a love letter that Stefan wrote and gave to Stromberg's mother, Diane (as reported by both Diane and Stromberg), when Diane and Stromberg's sister, Michelle, and several of his friends went to the West Walnut Lane apartment to collect Stromberg's things. This occurred shortly before the murders.

These murders made national news. *Hard Copy* television series did a segment interviewing Stromberg at the urging of his first lawyer, Vladimir Zdrok.

The *Courier-Journal* of Louisville, Kentucky, the city that Stefan and her family called home, published a story titled, "Ex-Louisville woman, her mother murdered in Philadelphia." She lived there with her parents before their divorce and her mother's remarriage and relocation to the Ft. Lauderdale area.

Another story that was buried in the *UPI* Archives dated April 30, 1996 was titled, "Horror Movie-maker Sought for Two Murders."

This story gives some additional details about Stromberg the actor and fitness trainer, as well as about the murder victims.

It adds specifics such as, "Police Capt. Patrick Dempsey said Stefan Stromberg, 30, had been slashed at least 20 times…"

A May 1, 1996 follow-up UPI article titled, "Actor Charged with 2 Murders Surrenders" stated, "Homicide Inspector Gerald Kane said Stromberg spent his time since the killings wandering through the woods in suburban Montgomery County. Kane said the murder weapon has not been recovered."

In an online piece written by David K. Frasier posted Thursday, February 27, 2014, titled, "Larry Stromberg – Washed in Blood", Frasier points out Stromberg's role in a horror-comedy flick from 1989 called, *Blades* as well as 'miniscule parts' in *12 Monkeys* and *Up Close & Personal,* two movies that were partially shot in Philly.

While his piece appears almost 20 years after the crime, it brings out several things worth noting here.

"Arguing his client was psychotic on the day of the killing, defense attorney Nino V. Tinari maintained Stromberg was the product of a mentally ill mother and a domineering father who had been molested as a child by babysitters and his mother's boyfriends."

Frasier writes that Tinari also stated that, "He [*Stromberg*] couldn't interact with women." Tinari said, "At age 30, he still played with dolls given to him at age 10."

On the other hand, Frasier notes, "Prosecutors presented a simpler theory of the case – the actor killed his wife and mother-in-law out of rage."

He goes on to say that Stromberg, after his conviction of first and second-degree murders and sentence of two life terms, has formed *The Redeemed Theater* while at Coal Township Prison. At the time of this article Stromberg "had written over 25 original plays for the prison population and the glory of God."

Currently, Stromberg is at S.C.I. Graterford where he has developed his ministry theater and joined in with the Lifers, Inc. group writing and performing his plays. He now has written over

60 plays, many of which can be found online at the prisons foundation website (*prisonsfoundation.org*).

*   *   *

5
NGRI & Appeals

There are a few notes of importance to the reader's understanding of this case. Mainly, what defense was used and how it is viewed by the State of Pennsylvania; and, the legal guidelines which affect the outcome of a murder trial.

The defense in this case was going to use the "Not Guilty by Reason of Insanity" (NGRI) plea. There are several rules or tests for the insanity plea used by the various States. They are: the M'Naghten rule, the Durham (Product) test (New Hampshire only), the Model Penal Code test (or the American Law Institute test), and the Guilty but Mentally Ill (GBMI) option.

Using an insanity defense brings about a change in the burden of proof, shifting it from the prosecution to the defense. This was brought about by the *Insanity Defense Reform Act* of 1984 (stemming from the attempted assassination of President Reagan).

Following is the standard definition used for the M'Naghten rule, which is the test that the State of Pennsylvania uses in such cases.

> Pennsylvania is one of the states that follow the M'Naghten (*McNaughton or M'Naughten*) rule, rather than the Model Standard set out by the American Law Institute (A.L.I.), which is:
> based on the 1843 British case of Daniel M'Naghten, a deranged woodcutter who attempted to assassinate the prime minister. He was acquitted, and the resulting standard is still used in 26 states in the U.S.: A defendant may be found not guilty by reason of insanity (*NGBRI*) if 'at the time of committing the act, he was laboring under such a defect of reason from disease of the mind as not to know the nature and quality of the act he was doing, or if he did know it, that he did not know what he was doing was wrong.'[1]

This rule is taken from a case where the defendant (Daniel M'Naghten) was tried before the British House of Lords for killing Edward Drummond, Prime Minister Robert Peel's secretary, mistaking him for the Prime Minister.[2]

One additional element to note here is that "in order for insanity to constitute a defense, a defendant must prove insanity by a preponderance of the evidence." [3]

This is significant because the standard used to reach a guilty verdict is normally 'beyond a reasonable doubt'. Here, to reach a not guilty verdict (NGRI) the threshold is much higher.

That may be one reason why only one percent of criminal cases use the insanity plea and, of those only one in four win.

Unfortunately for Stromberg, his was one of the three out of four that lose using this argument.

Another unfortunate thing for him was that Pennsylvania is not one of the states that uses the M'Naghten rule modified to "include a provision for a defendant suffering under 'an irresistible impulse' which prevents him from being able to stop himself from committing an act that he knows is wrong."[4]

From his account, that is what he experienced. He felt an irresistible impulse that he could not overcome; and, that is what he believes led him to commit this horrible act.

One important note: States have great latitude to enact and/or reform their own criminal and penal codes, subject to the "due process" and "cruel and unusual punishment" clauses of the U.S. Constitution.

Having failed at his attempt to obtain a NGRI (sometimes written as NGBRI) verdict, Stromberg's appeal was based on several other alleged major errors made during the trial (as cited in the appeal brief).

Stromberg, just as any convicted criminal in the United States, has the right to make at least one appeal. So, an appeal was filed. Rules and procedures for appeal vary from State to State, so here, only the procedural basics that apply to Pennsylvania will be discussed.

Did Stromberg receive a fair trial or even have competent representation throughout the whole process, from pre-trial to the several courts of appeal? The following notes might lead one to a possible answer.

A few words concerning the procedure in a murder case.

The criminal justice process starts with the arrest, during which suspects must be informed by the police about their rights while in custody. This process is known as the 'Miranda warning'.

The heart of the Miranda right is the right to be advised by a lawyer who is present once questioning has begun.

Next, there is a preliminary hearing or arraignment. At the arraignment, the District Attorney formally charges the defendant. The defendant, with the aid of his lawyer, voices his plea to the judge and the terms of bail are then decided by the judge.

Bail can be denied where the D.A. and judge decide there is a substantial risk of flight. Bail can also be denied if the judge decides an allegedly violent defendant will hurt himself or someone else.

Generally, there is then an incubation period wherein the state and the defense prepare their arguments.

Next, the D.A. seeks an indictment from a grand jury. A judge then schedules a guilt trial, unless the defendant waives his right to a jury trial; after which the trial proceeds.

Once the guilt trial is over, the jury decides whether the defendant is guilty "beyond a reasonable doubt" or not guilty.

In Pennsylvania's bifurcated system, there is a separate sentencing phase. In the Stromberg case, he was charged with first degree murder, hence a jury was required to take part in the sentencing.

Under Pennsylvania's criminal procedures, judges are not allowed to let a "hung" jury stop the process. Instead, in first degree murder sentencing hearings, when the jury cannot arrive at a unanimous decision on the sentence, the law requires the judge to sentence the defendant to life without parole. The final part of the process is the appeal(s).

Every person convicted of a crime in the United States has the right to at least one appeal before one or more appellate court(s). These special courts utilize panels of judges that rely on the facts decided by the trial court. They only decide questions of law.

Stromberg's trial ran from May 21 through June 9, 1997, a little more than one year after the murders.

After the case was decided by the Court of Common Pleas and the sentence imposed on June 9, 1997, Stromberg filed an appeal to the Superior Court of Pennsylvania, dated June 27, 1997.

The appeal court, made up of a three-judge panel, went through the eight points (as enumerated by Stromberg's attorney) of the appeal to determine whether or not the appeal had merit enough to warrant a new trial or reversal of charges.

This appeal, decided by a panel of three judges, included: Judge Popovich, Judge Hudock and President Judge Emeritus Cercone.

While in a criminal trial, the prosecution must prove beyond a reasonable doubt the defendant's guilt to a judge or jury, in an appeal the appellant bears the responsibility to demonstrate any error made in the original conviction.

Following is an abbreviated account of the points made in Stromberg's appeal to the Superior Court of Pennsylvania:

The appeal presented **eight points**, attempting to demonstrate errors in the original trial.

First, was the notion that the evidence in the trial demonstrated that he was legally insane at the time of the murders. The appellate court affirmed Judge Glazer's resolution of this issue.

The **second** point brought up the testimony given by Lilly, as well as Long, as to the hearsay evidence of "other crimes" that Stromberg had raped Stefan. Judge Glazer had allowed this in the original trial, with a caution to the jury. Again, they affirmed on the basis of the Trial Court in this matter.

The **third** argument concerned the color photographs of the nude bodies of the victims. The argument here was whether the Trial Court erred in permitting these photos showing the 'gruesome injuries' being shown to the jury as part of the medical examiner's testimony. This Court again agreed that Judge Glazer had set forth the accurate legal standard with regards to the admission of the color slides at the trial

Four, the appeal stated that the Trial Court was in error for denying a motion for a mistrial due to the medical examiner's statement that she "believed that the defendant had the specific intent to kill the victims." She testified that the injuries inflicted in this case indicated, "It's as though someone really intended for these people to die."

Once again, the Appellate Court agreed with Judge Glazer's assessment that the improper comment of the medical examiner did not rise to the level of prejudice that would require the Court to grant a mistrial.

The next argument (**five**) was that the Trial Court's charge to the jury concerning the defense's burden of proof for use of the insanity plea was improper and incomplete. This statement (or charge) concerned the explanation or definition of the phrase "preponderance of evidence."

The Court found the Trial Court's instruction to the jury concerning an insanity defense 'adequate'.

Point number **six** specifically pointed out the that the prosecutor's closing argument was unduly prejudicial. His remarks, that Stromberg was "...draped in the American flag...", etc., were not merely hyperbole, but prejudiced the jury. The Court again affirmed the Trial Court's judgment.

Seven focused on whether the Trial Court erred in allowing the jury to see the defendant's medical records. These records included the psychological and psychiatric reports, as well as the prison records.

Here again, the Court found that the Trial Court did not err in allowing the jury to take certain medical records out with them.

And the final point (**eight**) questioned whether Stromberg received the effective assistance of his attorneys, both Zdrok and Tinari.

It is important to note here that there is a **three-part test** to whether counsel is effective or not. **First**, the defendant must show that there is some merit to his or her claim of ineffective counsel. **Second**, he or she must show that counsel had no "reasonable basis for undertaking or failing to undertake the act or omission in question."

And, finally (**third**), that the act or omission caused the outcome to be different than had the counsel not added or omitted the thing in question.[5]

Regarding Zdrok, the Appellate Court found that, in balance, his entering into a business agreement with Stromberg and having him appear on *Hard Copy* did not constitute a claim of ineffective counsel.

As to the second part of this claim, that of Tinari's ineffective counsel, the Court found the allegations meritless.

With that, the Superior Court of Pennsylvania declined to grant relief for the defendant and they affirmed the judgment of the sentence.

Following this appeal, heard by the Superior Court of Pennsylvania, a petition for allowance was presented to the Supreme Court of Pennsylvania. This was petitioned in 1999, but not heard by the court.

The petition for allowance of appeal presented by Daniel A. Rendine, Esq. of Rendine and McConeghy of Philadelphia to the Supreme Court of Pennsylvania gave an account from the time of the murders through the original trial and sentencing. It focused on four major points:

I. The evidence was insufficient to sustain the guilty verdict as to all charges because the evidence showed that the defendant was legally insane at the time of this incident

II. The Honorable Trial Court erred in permitting hearsay evidence regarding the alleged rape of Stefan Stromberg by the defendant as this evidence was impermissible hearsay and concerned "other crimes evidence"

III.   The prosecutor's closing argument was unduly prejudicial

IV.   The defendant [had not] received the effective assistance of trial counsel[6]

*   *   *

6
Friends & Associates
July 12-14, 2016

These demons were real, whether sent by Satan himself or just the devil within us all that we call free will.

On Wednesday, July 13, 2016, prior to meetings with Stromberg's friends and associates, Larry Kirschner, Norman Macera and Sal DaRigo, about five hours was spent interviewing Stromberg at S.C.I. Graterford. It was fortunate to be allowed to have this conversation in a small room with a table and several chairs, since most visitors were in a large, noisy room together.

After our meeting with Stromberg where he discussed his life events from childhood to the present, a visit downtown to the courthouse to view the trial transcripts was made.

A large box was laid on the floor next to a table that was surrounded by a U-shaped sofa. In the box was a 1,000+ page trial transcript from the guilt and penalty phases of Stromberg's trial.

With such a vast amount of testimony and procedural text we were able to only scratch the surface; but enough to get a real sense of how the trial went and who the major players were. With two of us poring over the pages we were able to focus on the critical pieces that would bring this part of the story to life. After a few hours of reading and note-taking we worked our way to the north side of town.

A dinner meeting had been previously arranged with a friend of Stromberg's. In this interview with Stromberg's long-time friend and videographer, Larry Kirschner, he talked about how Stromberg was a nice, gentle man. He was also good looking and, while he attracted many women, he was an honorable single young man and didn't take advantage of these situations as many men in his position would have. Kirschner remarked, "He was also a very spiritual guy."

Kirschner remembered, "One time when Larry and I had gone to Center City where his father worked at a pizza parlor, I was struck at how the father tolerated the verbal abuse of the shop owner when he did some minor thing not to his liking; something as minute as putting too many mushrooms on a pizza. I was amazed that his father mildly took the abuse without any seeming anger."

He noted that this was the same kind of timidity and demeanor that he saw with Stromberg himself in several situations.

When pressed for any example of a temper, Kirschner admitted, "I have seen Larry become a bit short with his mother at times; but, I can understand why, given how demanding and controlling she could be."

He discussed Stromberg's acting ability and stated, "I believe Larry had talent and might have gone far had he been from a background where he could have gone to college and develop this talent. He was a very hard worker and I think that 'he would have cleaned toilets to make a buck.' Like his father, he had a strong work ethic; and like his father he needed his wife to work so that they could support themselves. And finances are often a big strain on a relationship."

The discussion over dinner in a German restaurant in Philadelphia led to many more topics, some Kirschner elaborated on from first-hand knowledge, some from what he had learned from Stromberg over the past 20 years.

He talked about the affairs Stromberg believed that Stefan had while married to him, which led to a pregnancy and ultimately to an abortion.

Like other friends and relatives of Stromberg's interviewed, Kirschner indicated that, "In my opinion, Larry just snapped; given the kind of person he appeared to be every day consistently, he would have never committed this heinous crime had he been in his right mind."

Stromberg's friends and associates agreed that (in their opinion) if not for the affair(s), pregnancy and abortion he would have been able to walk away from this bad marriage. But all of this plus her pulling him back after pushing him away constantly, coupled with a lifetime of emotional, physical and sexual abuse from his childhood onward, was too much for him to deal with. This, they believe, caused him to hear voices directing him to the only outcome that was available to him.

Kirschner discussed some aspects of the trial, having attended several days of the guilt and sentencing phases. He pointed out that the last day of the trial when the verdict was announced was on a Friday. The following Monday was the only day for the sentencing phase.

He noted, "Whether everyone was exhausted from this long and arduous trial [*May 21-June 9, 1997*] or just ready to go home and be done with it because it was a Friday, the jury came out with the verdict in a very short time. Larry was found guilty of first degree murder. The sentencing hearing was started and concluded within a few hours on June 9th."

He continued, "The jury was unable to reach a verdict so the Court [*Judge Gary Glazer*] imposed the sentence following Pennsylvania guidelines."

Stromberg was given two consecutive life sentences for the murders, to which 120-240 months was added for the burglary charge; to be served consecutively to the second-degree murder sentence. No additional sentence was imposed for the PIC (possession of an instrument of crime) and contempt (his violation of the protection order) charges.

One thing that struck us at dinner that night was the fact that during the penalty phase there were few character witnesses called, and only the two expert witnesses (Drs. Kessel and O'Brien). Only a handful, who could show some mitigating circumstances that might preclude the death penalty, were called.

59

These other witnesses might have been able to shed some light on whether he would be likely to do this same kind of thing again.

Yet, despite this, there were people lined up outside the courtroom that were willing to testify to Stromberg's character, and professionals who would have been there had they been called. But none were, except for Drs. Kessel and O'Brien.

Possibly the length of the guilt phase of the trial and the fact that it was the beginning of a new week that made this weary jury unable to come to a decision as to the penalty. Or possibly some on the jury weren't convinced that it was premeditated, and that maybe he had snapped.

But whatever the reasoning, as Kirschner stated, "While it was an awful thing to have murdered two people, many others have been given much less time for the same or worse offenses."

He also stated that the judge, who can make a closing statement once the trial and sentencing is complete, excoriated Stromberg calling him a horrible person and the scum of the earth, among other things. This was reported by several people who were present at the trial and heard the judge's remarks. They all indicated that they were in shock at what he said and how he said it.

One aspect of the prosecution's case that Kirschner pointed out that seemed to make a big impression at the trial was the fact that Stromberg had a half hour bus ride from his new apartment to the apartment at West Walnut Lane where Stefan and Paula were packing for Stefan's move to Florida with her mother.

This time, plus what Stromberg himself described as what seemed like almost an hour lurking in the bushes just outside the apartment, should have been ample time for him to change his mind and not kill these two women.

That is, had it not been for his disturbing dreams and his hearing voices getting stronger telling him that he must do it!

These voices had been in his head for days now, according to his account. He was free to move on if he could only release himself from the grip these demons had on him.

Kirschner talked about *Spiritual Warfare*, "This was the film that Larry had been working on right up to the murders. At that time, it was two separate horror flicks, *Horrorscope* and *Heavenbound*. Larry, after his incarceration at S.C.I. Coal Township, decided that the films had to be completed and had the idea of combining them. Since they were not complete (less than half finished at this point), he called and asked me to complete it for him."

Kirschner agreed to complete this horror film with one condition "I told him I would complete the film, but it must send a positive message, one that will hopefully prevent people from committing crimes against one another (smiling as he reflected on his conversation with Stromberg). A horror movie with a real message, an unusual concept."

Stromberg agreed and work on its completion began. Kirschner recounted, "There were many obstacles in the way, such as completing the film without Stromberg, who was the main character in it! And it wasn't even half done."

Slowly, and through the U.S. mail and sometimes by telephone Stromberg detailed how he envisioned the completion of the movie, scene by scene. This, coupled with Kirschner's filmmaking skill and ingenuity, made it all come together. After twenty years in the making, *Spiritual Warfare* was completed. The film, narrated by Stromberg's uncle Nick Mamallis, was entered in an independent filmmakers' film festival in Los Angeles in the fall of 2016 and is now available on *Vimeo.com*.

In viewing this film, there seemed to be striking parallels between the characters in the movie, Von and Eddie (father and son) Kraven, and Stromberg in terms of the near strangulation of Stefan in real life and the girl in the film. Also, the stabbing of the girl in the film with the stabbing deaths of both Stefan and her mother, Paula.

Other things seemed eerily similar between the two, but Kirschner confesses that while one may find a little similarity, there is no real parallel that he finds – and he produced it!

There may not be, but in reading the trial transcript it is curious that Tinari (Stromberg's trial attorney), made a point of bringing up the character of Von Kraven during his presentation, saying that Stromberg (in his twisted mind at the time) assumed the role of Von Kraven and murdered his wife (and mother-in-law) just as Von Kraven had murdered in the film (*Horrorscope*, at that time).

While discussing this unlikely aspect of the film and connection or lack of it with the trial, Kirschner brought up an interesting point about Stromberg's attorney and his recent past.

Kirschner stated, "I believe that, although Tinari was presented with a plea bargain that would have given Larry 40-80 years instead of possibly life without parole or the death penalty, Larry never knew about this offer. Kirschner (as do others) believes that Tinari wanted this to go to trial believing he could win a NGRI verdict. As they say, 'There's no way this ain't going to trial!'."

Kirschner also talked about one of Stromberg's plays concerning prison life that was performed at the Philadelphia Fight Center, *Life Behind the Razor Wire*. It was read on stage by former inmates and was well received by the audience.

He noted, as have others, that Stromberg has written over 60 plays, some of which have been performed on stage at both S.C.I. Coal Township (where he spent the first 19 years of his incarceration) and S.C.I. Graterford (where he now resides).

Kirschner pointed out Stromberg's role as a model prisoner in both institutions.

He related that, "He had the job of cleaning the Superintendent's office at Coal Township and earned a single cell there after rooming with another man for five years. He also earned a single cell at Graterford where he works in the staff dining hall."

Kirschner stated that, in his discussions with Stromberg, "He knows he has ruined his life, but he accepts it."

He also stated emphatically that, "Everyone who knew Larry liked him."

In a closing note he said, "I have read many of Larry's plays and, as they are all about life in prison, I suggested that he write something different, maybe a comedy. And maybe someday he will."

After the meeting with Kirschner, across town at a small diner a later meeting with two other former friends of Stromberg, Norman Macera and Sal DaRigo had been scheduled. Because of the unusual amount of traffic in Philadelphia (due to the Democrat

National Convention to be held in just over a week from this visit) the meeting had to be pushed back. However, these two true friends were glad to wait because of their loyalty to their old friend, Larry Stromberg.

This meeting with Macera and DaRigo at a diner on the east side of town shortly before 10 pm was marked by an interesting conversation.

DaRigo is an actor who did some work with Stromberg, and a friend to him throughout the years, while Macera is an actor/filmmaker and a friend to Stromberg and DaRigo for many years. He has worked with both men on films.

DaRigo talked about the night before the murders when he and another friend of Stromberg's, Pete (not his real name), were with Stromberg at his apartment on Elmwood Ave. A pained expression glazed over DaRigo's rugged, time-worn visage as he began his journey back to that night.

"Larry was the nicest, gentlest guy; but he wasn't himself that night. He was out of it, strange acting. We tried to talk him down, you know, get him calm and back to his normal self. But he was gone."

The conversation continued with Macera chiming in with his take on Stromberg, agreeing that he was just that nice of a guy.

"He would walk 10 miles through snow and ice for a friend – and he has. He is that kind of a friend."

Macera talked about the *Hard Copy* interview. He had heard about it and told Stromberg not to do it, but Zdrok (Stromberg's attorney at the time) and Stromberg's mother, Diane, said that they thought he should. It turned out that Macera was right.

Whether it was reasonable to take that interview and make a diagnosis that Stromberg was sane at the time of the murders is a point of contention to Macera and DaRigo. But it made for a good story at the time – at least for Zdrok and *Hard Copy*.

Or as DaRigo put it (quoting), "Don't let the facts get in the way of a good story!" He, being an actor, attributed it to Alfred Hitchcock, but I believe it was first said by Mark Twain.

Neither DaRigo nor Macera were able to go to any of the trial.

*   *   *

7

Diane's Story & Family Memories

In conversations with Diane Stromberg, Stromberg's mother, she told of her past and that of her husband and children.

*   *   *

Growing up was a painful time for Larry and Michelle. They went through a great deal of turmoil during their first 18 years, and I suppose, due to my own difficult childhood.

But, I guess I should start at the beginning – my beginning.

I grew up Diane Mamallis, in a family that included my mother, Clara, father, Nicholas, and an older brother, Nick. My life was chaotic at times, which may have led me to the life fraught with its own imbalance that I brought to my marriage and family.

My mother, and father had their troubles as well. While Nick (my older brother) and I lived in Baltimore with our parents, our mother had an affair.

Our parent's marriage had been a traditional Greek one (that is, an arranged marriage). She was very young; younger than the man she was to marry. She neither knew him well, nor was in love with him, which may have been a cause leading her to have the affair.

This affair led to their divorce, and our father got custody of Nick and me. He took us to Millbourne, PA, a town outside of Philadelphia, where he became a captain on the police force.

In order to get out of the marriage (in the eyes of the church) our mother had to travel to New York City to meet with a Greek Bishop to arrange for the divorce. The state awarded our custody to our father.

My father remarried to a woman who had children of her own from a previous marriage. She also had a brother who sexually abused me. I was just a young girl at the time.

His new wife was cruel to me and, after my father drowned in a suspicious boating accident on a nearby lake, she locked me out of the house. I wasn't too upset about being locked out given my circumstances.

My mother, on the other hand, had remarried a man named Jack Tidball, who together had a daughter they named Ramona – Nick's and my half-sister. This was a good union for our mother and Jack alike.

While Nick and I were still young and living near Philadelphia (before our father died), our mother would travel from Baltimore in an attempt to see us. Since she was not allowed to visit with us, she had to be satisfied to secretly watch us at play and only from a distance. We were never aware of this at the time.

Around the time that our father died, my brother, Nick, had moved out to start a family of his own; sometime in 1963 or 64.

Soon my life became somewhat of a Cinderella story, before the prince's arrival. It was then, as a very young woman I met and married John Lawrence Stromberg, Larry Sr., a man my senior by almost 10 years (much like my mother's first marriage). He was the prince to the rescue.

We fell in love and he swept me away from my life of misery. Larry Sr. owned a pizza shop at that time. Unfortunately, we both were dreamers; he only wanted to be in love and work to provide for his family, but neither of us saw the reality of our lives. In his eyes, I could do no wrong, no matter how much I abused his love.

In this gallant effort to take me away from my predicament and because we were in love, we married. Larry and his sister, Michelle, were our first two children. Later came Shawn and Diane, who both died in infancy. Their deaths tore us apart. I was especially effected by the loss. I suppose I snapped; what mother wouldn't? Both so young and both in a short period of time. This began a downslide in our lives together.

Tragedy seemed to follow us around. Sometime early in our marriage, I was driving down a street in Philadelphia when I struck a young girl while the girl's mother and aunt standing nearby witnessed it. The child died shortly after, in the hospital. Of course, the mother was devastated by this, but so was I. This memory plagued me for many years.

I was never charged since the child's mother and aunt both saw the girl run out in front of me, without there being anytime for me to stop or swerve, and they agreed that I was not at fault. But that doesn't make the painful memory any less.

Even though I wasn't charged, while the investigation was going on I had to come up with bail in order not to be put in jail. Having no money for this myself, a family member who had a row house in Upper Darby put it up for my bond.

Coincidently, our daughter, Michelle, was hit by a car at one point in her early life; she survived, however, with only minor injuries.

When Larry Sr. and I were first married, life was hard. We often found we had to rely on family members to get by, even sometimes for a place to live.

During one of these times, before the children came along, we lived with one of his siblings in their two-bedroom row house. Their basement had a pile of things that belonged to us that my sister-in law said, "Looked like the mud-mountain in the movie, *Close Encounters...*" This stay lasted only a few weeks as it became difficult living together; so, we moved out.

Another incident, early in our marriage, occurred when we again had no place to live, so we moved in to Larry Sr.'s parents' house. One day, my mother-in-law and I got into an argument and I pushed her a little too hard, sending her to the ground breaking her leg. One of Larry Sr.'s brothers had to carry his mother out of the house to take her to the hospital. We had to move out once more.

This was all a part of the family life young Larry and Michelle were raised in. But it was only a part of the tragedy of their lives at this point.

After Shawn's and Diane's (our third and fourth children) deaths, I began a relationship with a man that I knew from the Philadelphia airport where I worked at the diner. He also worked at the airport and we began to see each other as well as ride to and from work together.

My relationship with Jon (not his real name) was a destructive one. I left my husband and moved in with Jon only to find that he would whip my two children with a bullwhip and abuse me as well; once even throwing me onto railroad tracks as we were riding together on the way to work.

I returned to my husband for a short time, but again left him; this time for Nashville to pursue my dream of becoming a country singer where I was offered a job as a backup singer by Hank Williams, Jr. I had visions of becoming a famous singer and one day would fulfill that dream, or so I thought. I had to turn the offer down because I couldn't be on the road touring with my two small children.

While in Nashville, my children and I lived with a woman named Christy (not her real name), who was the mistress of a famous (married) country singer.

It was then that Larry and Michelle were sexually and physically abused by babysitters. This was only the first of many times that they had to endure this kind of abuse at the hands of babysitters and other adults.

Christy's two teenage daughters watched my young children while Christy and I worked, trying to eke out a living. Unknown to either Christy or me, while we worked, her two daughters would molest my two little children. One of the girls would watch while the other made Larry and Michelle perform sexual acts on her.

Seeing no road to stardom, I finally came to my senses and took my two children home to their father and back to the dysfunction that they had known all their lives. But, at the time, I was unaware of what my children had been through. In fact, it wasn't until years later, and only after a second babysitter abused them, that I learned of this horrible experience.

And as my own dream of becoming a famous singer faded, I began to build a dream world for my children. They would become famous actors.

After returning from Nashville, Larry Sr. and I tried again to create a calm and happy home; but this was never to be.

The same chaos and turmoil which controlled our lives haunted us still. In my heart, I loved my husband, but I wanted more out of life than he could provide; I was spinning out of control, and so was the rest of my family.

Larry and Michelle were innocent victims of our inability to create a safe and stable environment for them. The predators seeing this, took advantage of it by molesting and abusing both of them for much of their childhood years; and without Larry Sr. or I even being aware of it until it was too late.

All of this went on without any intervention or professional help until my two children reached adulthood and began to self-destruct, each on their own path; both in destructive relationships.

While Michelle had her own demons to fight, Larry was trying to control his. His acting and working out seemed to help him live in a somewhat calm and happy manner. None of us could see that his demons were at work inside, waiting to come out – but they did.

As young children, Larry and Michelle saw Larry Sr. and my many arguments, while living in a house in turmoil, and constantly moving from apartment to apartment and job to job.

*　　　*　　　*

One family member reported, "Larry and Michelle ran wild as children; undisciplined and unruly, but sweet children nonetheless. The house was in total disarray, filled with boxes of 'stuff', animals running all around and trash everywhere. Larry Sr. and Diane had it hard. They sometimes lived with relatives, even after the first two children came along. It was very hard for a young married couple to have to uproot so often, especially with two small children."

But there were good memories that the family shared, and remember to this day.

Stromberg's aunt Ramona remarked in a conversation one evening about Stromberg, the happy 4-year-old.

She said, "I can recall those days as if they were just yesterday when we would all go to Larry Sr.'s pizza shop and watch little Larry put on a play for his family. He performed his plays as we watched in amazement at his love for acting, even at that young of an age."

Stromberg laughed as he confirmed his aunt's remembrance at how he had always loved performing and making others laugh and be happy.

He remarked, "I would sing songs and play a character or just recite a little rhyme I had committed to memory. Sometimes just act goofy, you know, to get a laugh. I loved making people smile and laugh."

And that love became a passion for him as he grew older; in fact, it became a means of escape from the cruelty that the world showed him.

This same passion was (in some small way) the cause of the failure of his marriage. He was married to the stage and screen and thought he could have a meaningful relationship with a woman, despite the long hours performing and filming; and doing all those things that he needed to do to feel fulfilled while trying to make a better life for himself and his bride.

That, coupled with a life of abuse and wounds that ran deep into his core, would never permit him to have a healthy relationship, especially with a woman as scarred as himself.

*   *   *

8

Death & Desolation

"… the beautiful memories I have with Stefan that mean so much to me always and forever."
Larry Stromberg (2016)

The solemn mood of the onlookers permeated the courtroom as the prosecution presented its case with passion and a plethora of witnesses and experts wagging their tongues and shaking their metaphoric fists in the air as if to say: *GUILTY!*

But, of course, guilty; the real question was, "Was he sane at the time of the murders?" All the while, as his blank gaze drifted in another world, Stromberg's thoughts were of Stefan, their short life together and the deep love he always had for her.

Confused by his own emotions, he reopened the memories, good and bad, that put him where he sat today.

* * *

Following is my story. The truth, and honest on all levels…

It's funny how history repeats itself. While my father, who was one of eight children, wanted only to live a peaceful and happy life, my mother, the second of two children of a man who had been a police captain of a small community outside of the Philadelphia area and a woman who suffered from depression, wanted more.

She wanted more out of life than my father had to offer her. She wanted to become a big-name singer and wanted her two children to become famous actors. And so, my sister, Michelle, and I went for acting lessons and our mother pursued her singing career.

As a boy, after the death of my brother, Shawn, and my sister, Diane, my mother and father separated due to my mother's infidelity. My mother moved in with her boyfriend Jon where me and Michelle were beaten by a bull whip many times. My mother left the man and my parents reconciled. But this didn't last long.

At this point my mother took me and my sister Michelle on the road to pursue a singing career.

She took us to Nashville, Tennessee where me and Michelle first experienced sexual, mental, emotional and physical abuse. Then she moved us back to Pennsylvania where a female baby sitter sexually abused me at least over 100 times as my mother was at work as a bartender. I was a 7-year-old having sexual relations with an 18-year-old woman. She would make my sister watch or run around the apartment naked. She would play with my private parts and make me perform oral sex on her. She tried to make me have sex with her, but being only a seven-year-old, I was not able to and she would become furious at me and yell obscenities.

The babysitter warned us that if we told anyone a cross would burn on our chests, which scared us into silence.

Finally, Michelle told our mother about the abuse and my mother fired her as a babysitter, but never pressed criminal charges. And me and Michelle never got help from the abuse. Our innocence as children was taken from us.

Once again, my mother went back to my dad. They opened a pizza restaurant and my mother continued her singing career.

As a young teenager, I started seeing my first girlfriend, Carrie (not her real name); I was on the wrestling team at the time. Her father, George (not his real name), molested me twice while driving me home after a date with his daughter. He told me he would kill me if I had intercourse with Carrie. He'd stalk me and taped my phone conversations with her. He would tell me my future from readings of tarot cards. After a few months, me and Carrie broke up. I was ashamed of the sexual abuse. I didn't tell anybody about the abuse for years.

My sister had her painful times as well. She became a drug addict, alcoholic, and had numerous abortions. She often ran away from home to be with boyfriends for days at a time. She had her own trauma, but that's her story to tell – if she chooses.

She once tried to kill our mother by sneaking up behind her at her workplace in the parking lot and smashing a brick over her head a dozen times. When they came up to get me, my mother's head was full of blood. Michelle was high and out of her mind. We all got in the car to pick up my father at the train station. My mother would not go to the hospital until we got our father. My mother told the doctor and nurses she fell down the steps. We kept it a family secret. Over the years, Michelle went on to try to commit suicide many times, and has been in prison and drug rehab. She's doing better now and has a beautiful daughter.

My mother's dream to be a successful singer all ended the day Michelle tried to kill her. It died. But my father still tried to keep the family together.

Despite these setbacks, my mother eventually did cut a demo album of songs in Boston. Some of the songs were even played on the radio. But that was the extent of her career.

I suppose it wouldn't have been so bad had it not been for the totality of the chaos. It was like being in a hurricane where only the eye (our dad) was calm and sunny. Everything else spun around us.

We had cats and dogs (I'm not sure how many), boxes of things all around the house, trash (some strewn around by the cats and dogs) all over the place and a chaotic schedule of babysitters, who sexually and physically molested both Michelle and me while my parents were at work.

It may, after all I've just related, seem strange, but I love my mother and always have. You could say we've had a stormy relationship most of our lives.

In every case of abuse by babysitters, when my mother would eventually find out, she would not press charges or even file a report with the police; instead we would run away from the problem. The counseling and treatment that we so desperately needed was denied us. We were left scarred for life with no help in trying to make us whole.

It was after the physical, sexual and emotional abuse over these early years of my young life that I made the promise to myself that it would never happen again. I would never be abused by anyone – ever. I began an intense and focused regimen that included physical and spiritual training. Lifting weights, playing sports and reading the Bible dominated my time.

As a young adult, my physical training paid off in several ways. I no longer felt the fear of being physically or sexually abused. My imposing new physique gave me the confidence that no one would be able to take advantage of me.

My training had also enabled me to excel in sports in school and in the schoolyard. I enjoyed games of physical agility and engaged in them whether as competition or just for fun. But my first love in the world of sports was wrestling. I competed on my high school team and practiced the moves and holds with a passion.

It was also during this time that I became more keenly interested in acting, so my mother enrolled me in classes.

*   *   *

His sister Michelle laughed as she reminisced about that period in their lives. She remarked, "He used to practice his wrestling moves on me. It would annoy me, but I loved my brother and, in a way, it was our way of bonding. Those were the 'good' times as I remember."

*   *   *

As I grew into my teen years, my mother and I continued to disagree. While I prayed every day, and tried to be a good son, she seemed to have her own idea of what I should do and with whom I should associate.

In my mother's eyes, any girl or woman (when I grew into manhood) was never good enough for me. I know many mothers believe that of their sons, but in my mother's case it was a mission, an obsession; maybe because of her infidelity to my father, or maybe she saw something in them that I didn't.

Nevertheless, she would call and threaten many of the women that I tried to date. Not just one call, but sometimes 30 or 40 calls.

I can say these things now because she and I have found the kind of mother-son relationship that we should always have had. Oddly enough, our relationship throughout my whole life has been a difficult one up until my incarceration.

It is sad to note that it took the death of two innocent people for us to see what was most valuable in life.

While I have just outlined some (yes, there was much more) of the things in my life that my mother either caused or allowed, there were many good times as well. Amidst the chaos and confusion, I can still remember with warm thoughts the times that we enjoyed as a family; the simple, happy times.

My mother has been through a lot in her life as well. Her story contains much hardship and tragedy. After I was born in 1966, my sister, Michelle, came along in 1967 and we were a family. Next came two other siblings – Shawn and Diane. But they both died as infants. Shawn, born in 1971, died of a defect in his esophagus at six months old; Diane, born in 1973, died of pneumonia at three months old. These were devastating blows to both of my parents, but especially to my mother who, after the death of my brother, Shawn, drifted away from my father. They both seemed to be going their separate ways at that time. It was a short time after the death of Diane that my mom had the affair with Jon.

Through it all, my dad would take her back each time. I don't think it was that she was a bad person or that he was a saint. Some people are just not meant to be together; bad chemistry, I guess. I suppose Stefan and I were the same, which explains why people that shouldn't get together often do, and almost certainly, with tragic results.

The deaths of my brother, Shawn, and sister, Diane, still sit firmly in my mind. Although I was still a young child at the time, their deaths only added to a life that was becoming increasingly more and more painful.

I'm a man serving a double life sentence for a crime I'm forever remorseful for. Forever. I have a broken heart. You see, I destroyed a family; I destroyed my family. For that I'm forever sorry that words can't express.

Yes, the devil is real. So is our Father in Heaven.

*   *   *

As my focus on the physical self, strengthening my body and learning the art of acting grew, I was also developing my spiritual being. Accepting Christ as my Lord and Savior came at a time when I decided to go to acting school in New York and Philadelphia.

I kept up my acting by taking classes at several acting schools. I also performed on stage and in film as opportunities arose. I had parts in many different films, made-for-TV movies, stage plays, etc. during this period in my life.

This was a very promising and productive time for me as I had roles in movies and on stage. I had roles in plays like *Death of a Salesman*, *Our Town*, *Richard the III* and *Arsenic and Old Lace*. My acting career was moving upward very quickly.

I also wrote, directed and starred in films of my own called, *Gruesome's Legend* and *Spiritual Warfare*.

Juxtaposed to this was my relationship with my family. As I began to meet more and different kinds of people due to my work in films and on stage, I also began to date some of the women I met. One, a woman named Jan (not her real name) that I liked a great deal, worked in the business and we began to date. In true form, my mother began to call the woman, threatening her and harassing her over and over until she was scared off. This, of course, led to battles between us.

I continued to live with my parents and focus on my acting career and taking care of my pets. I dated, but nothing serious, partly because I was afraid of the outcome if I did.

Besides my mother's interference with any serious relationship I had with a woman, I never felt sexually adequate. My early childhood years of sexual abuse had made me feel "different" and I prayed that the right woman would come along to fulfill that part of my life. That was probably one of the reasons I allowed my mother to drive any girlfriends away.

I worked as a personal trainer at *Riverside Fitness and Racquet Center*; now called *The Aquatic and Fitness Center at Riverside* in Bala Cynwyd, PA.

81

Many [women] asked me out on dates. Married women. But, as a Christian, I knew that being with a married woman was wrong in God's holy eyes.

One time I was asked by a friend of mine to have sex with his wife as he would watch with pleasure. He offered to pay me a thousand dollars to do this. I turned down the offer.

I wanted to marry a woman I loved. Well, after a period of time a woman came into my life. Her name was Stefan Broude. She worked part time at the *Fitness Center* and had a full-time job at *Temple Hospital* as a Social Worker

While Stefan was pursuing a career working at Temple University Hospital and a side business making and selling jewelry, I had yet to establish myself in a very difficult profession to break into. I had regular work, some of which was in major motion pictures such as *Rocky V*, *Up Close and Personal* and *Money for Nothing*, and on stage in plays like, *Tony and Tina's Wedding* and *I Love My Wife*. I also had a lead role in a horror film called, *Blades*, in addition to working on my own horror films.

Acting and writing takes me to a special place that words can't describe. It sets me free from my deepest fears and I feel like I'm riding the light that guides me beyond myself. I know that this may sound crazy, but it's true.

*　　　*　　　*

Wife & Mother

Unfortunately, when Stromberg and Stefan met they began both a beautiful and horrible relationship. When two people are attracted to each other the magic doesn't know the baggage each carries with them. It doesn't consider the consequences of a decision to follow that magic. It never accounts for the results that happen after the magic is gone; or worse yet, the actions one or both might take as the magic turns to jealousy and rage. That is what happened in this relationship.

Add to that mix a mother who wants so desperately to control her child's life; even after he or she has grown up; essentially "for their own good", and you have the beginning of a tumultuous relationship that never really had a chance to blossom.

In her own words, Diane stated that she felt that none of these girls (women) that Stromberg was seeing was good enough for him. She said she saw them as tramps and women that would keep him from, what she believed would be, becoming a star.

She especially hated Stefan because she could see that this one was not just a woman he would date, but someone he was falling in love with. She was a real threat and definitely not good enough for her son. Diane believed that Stefan was trashy, a tramp who slept around casually with many men and was not at all suitable for a good Christian man like her son. He was too immature to be getting married, as one of Stromberg's other relatives put it.

Diane once related to a family member that she was going to break this marriage up no matter what it took. There was even a conspiracy theory within the family that Diane was the one who committed the murders. But we know differently; Stromberg's dying mother-in-law identified him as the assailant and he confessed as well.

But possibly, that theory was more metaphoric than realistic. It's not hard to see that death is one of the ways to break up a marriage in her remark, "Whatever it took."

For Diane's part, while she didn't commit the actual crime, she would call Stefan up and threaten her.

That's when Stromberg had to decide; did he love Stefan enough to go against his mother, possibly for the first time; or was she just another woman that he was not willing to fight for?

Stromberg stated, "My mother treated me like I betrayed her; my father was okay with everything. My mother became depressed and hated my wife with a passion. It took time for my mother and my wife to find a place of peace within themselves. In the struggle, I was torn to make my mother happy and like Stefan. I moved out for a few days from my wife back to my parents' house. I was confused and troubled by all the failed relationships."

These words resonated over and over during our many conversations. In some ways, he seemed more than haunted by the past; he seemed trapped in it. To hear him replay their relationship and all its turmoil, it was as if he was reliving each moment again and again.

There seemed to be a definite duality to him. On the one hand, he lived to write, act and produce his plays of salvation and God's mercy. On the other, the darker side, his past was like a tornado swirling around him; spinning with the ugly past.

And why not, one might suppose; from childhood through the time of the murders his life was in a constant state of flux.

They did things together like any loving couple. But there was still anger toward Diane on Stefan's part, as there was on Diane's toward Stefan's as well.

Stromberg wrote that Stefan once even said that she wished his mother was dead. Regrettably, he was so angered by this that he struck Stefan.

This might just have been a foreshadowing of the end that resulted. It seems that Stromberg felt the strong need to please both women in his life, but was unable to please either. It was a situation that he felt no control over and, yet, was just as responsible for.

We are certainly a product of our environment, but a product of our genetics first and foremost. And, while Stromberg seems to be easy going and even a pushover at times, much like his dad, he also has an intensity and determination like his mother.

He had an inward growing need to live a good Christian life in a world showing him the worst it had to offer. Sexual and physical abuse, emotional abuse, parents in constant strife, a home that was shifting from place to place and filled with chaos and turmoil.

Not only was Stromberg dealing with a mother who was pulling him one way and a wife who was pulling him the other, he was dealing with the demons in his head. Those demons preyed upon a life created by a childhood of abuse and chaos, a naïveté that made him a target for predators.

85

As Stromberg related this, one could hear the pain in his voice, not only for his bad choices, but specifically for the rapes, and mostly for what followed. The downward spiral of their relationship was gaining blinding speed.

For anyone who has ever been in a relationship, it's always a matter of give and take. You sometimes must give in to the other person to make the relationship work.

What kept the two of them in this relationship? What drove them to abuse each other and then attempt to 'make it work'? Maybe for sex; maybe for any show of affection that each might give the other. But constantly rewarding and punishing can suck the life out of a person. That's what is happening when affection and sex are used to pull someone in after pushing them away.

*   *   *

9
Love & Marriage

As the trial moved along, I sat in sober silence and faded back to a better time; a time when I was first in love. Stefan and I met and fell in love quickly, as so many people do.

It was in 1993 when Stefan Broude and I first met. The first time she walked up to me was when I was at work at the *Riverside Aquatic and Fitness Center* in Bala Cynwyd and she said, "Hello" to me and smiled. I remember that moment vividly.

As a trainer and actor, I was used to working with beautiful women, but there was something special about this woman; something that attracted me to her like no other. We talked, mostly her because I was too taken by her to get the words out. I just smiled and tried to act 'cool', like my muteness was me playing the role of the strong, silent type – instead of it being due to my not knowing what to say to the woman I would soon ask to marry me. In fact, it only took a matter of six weeks before that would happen.

But we were from two very different worlds. Stefan was from a prominent Jewish family in Louisville, Kentucky, where her father was the head of finance at *Jewish Hospital*, and I, the son of parents who at times each managed different restaurants and at other times my dad made pizza in a pizzeria and my mom was a waitress at an airport diner.

Stefan traveled to Philadelphia after graduation from high school to attend *Temple University* and then, after earning a Master's Degree, began a career in social work at *Temple Hospital*. Stefan was also very entrepreneurial minded and started her own jewelry business out of our apartment.

For extra money, she also took on a part-time job as a hostess and waitress at *Long's Gourmet Chinese Restaurant* downtown. That was where she met and became friends with Phan Long, the owner, and an Asian cook at the restaurant that Stefan admitted to having an affair with and, at one point, claimed was the father of her aborted baby.

We were not so different in one respect. While she may have been the child of a stable, well-to-do family and I the product of a not-to-stable and not so well off one, we were both driven to be successful in our careers.

That obsession with career was part of my undoing. While my mother was (in large part) the cause (whether intentionally or unintentionally) of much of the trauma I suffered in life, I was now spinning out of control due to my own choices and didn't even realize it. As with many people, my mom was living with her own demons.

I can say these things and more because I blame only myself for my crime. My mother, with all her faults, loved my sister and me very much. While she always wanted the best for us, she sometimes went about it the wrong way, or without regard as to how her actions would impact others – like my father.

I have related all of this, I guess, so that all the things that I am about to tell you about Stefan and myself makes any sense.

While together we created the 'perfect storm', apart we were lonely, searching for that someone to make us complete. We were each other's soul mate – and each other's worst nightmare.

But there were good times; and when it was good it was very good. And it was the simple things I remember most.

I remember the night, shortly after we first met in 1993, that I went to her apartment. It was in June and the weather was warm. We went for a swim in the pool behind her apartment and then had ice cream. That apartment at 251 West Walnut Lane would soon become our home and later the scene of her murder.

I can still remember spending a carefree weekend at the Jersey shore with her and some of her friends. We walked along the boardwalk at night as the cool ocean breeze danced about our wind-burned faces. We walked together, hand-in-hand, and talked for hours unaware of anything else but each other.

And this would have been a magical moment had it not been for one thing that seemed odd to me at the time, and later stood out more and more as a portent of what was to come in our relationship.

Her old boyfriend, Bob, (not his real name) was staying in the same rented shore house with her other friends and us that weekend. Despite this, we became a steady couple.

As we saw each other almost constantly, that is, whenever we weren't working, and sometimes when we were, we became more and more in love. She would come to see me at the fitness center when I worked in the evening and, even from a distance as she approached, I could see she looked forward to being with me, if those moments together were only for a short time; just as much as I'm sure she saw in my face that I looked forward to her visits.

Six weeks is a very short time to get to know a person, but we had spent so much time together awake and asleep that we felt that we knew each other and that we were both ready to make our relationship the only relationship we cared to have.

That's what love does to you. I was committed to her, just as my father had been to my mother. I guess I learned a lot of good along with the bad throughout my childhood. And one thing I do remember is seeing the light in my father's eyes when he was with my mom. I felt the same about Stefan.

We went to visit her father in Louisville, Kentucky and we made a choice together, to get married. So much of what we did was spontaneous; and I suppose spontaneity has its place, but unfortunately for us there was too much of that.

Once in Louisville and decided we were going to marry, we went out and bought our weddings rings. We bought them at a pawnshop. We laughed about it; but the rings were just the symbol of our love and commitment to each other, not the love and commitment itself.

With that done and the wedding planned we went to a drive-in theater to see a double feature that weekend. I rented a tuxedo for the wedding ceremony, which took place in a park. Stefan was a most beautiful bride in her purple wedding dress, and she felt it, as purple was her favorite color. Our wedding day was magnificent with purple flowers and the night at a grand hotel downtown. But most of all, we adored each other and this day celebrated how we felt toward one another. Everyone at the wedding could see that. That was Saturday, September 7, 1993, the happiest day of our lives.

There are many good memories of our time together. It almost sounds psychotic, but I try only to remember our love and happiness and forget about the infidelity and arguments. And I will never forget what I did, nor get over the loss of two wonderful people because of me.

At Christmas time, we would go out and find the perfect tree to decorate our home. While it was a simple back apartment in a once beautiful mansion, it was our home. Even though Stefan was Jewish and I a practicing Christian we celebrated Christmas together.

We bathed in the glow of the many lights that brightened the tree and reflected in the dazzling array of ornaments which punctuated the holiday spirit we felt as we sat on the floor with our two dogs, Spartagus and Bandit; this gave us pause to reflect on the many joys that made our lives together special.

Stefan even had one special ornament, a beautiful purple one that she carefully placed where everyone could see it; after all, purple was her favorite color. She would even wear the purple choke that she loved so much as we decorated our tree.

And our apartment, in all its Christmas glory, was a testament to our belief that this time of year was a time of hope, faith and the renewal of our commitment to one another. Sadly, there were only three short Christmas's that we shared together. Now I share it with only a memory.

During that brief time, we would drive to my parents in Lancaster, Pennsylvania to visit. I remember Stefan and I lying in the back of our pickup truck and staring up at the stars above as they illuminated the night sky. We would lie there without talking, holding each other and feeling the beauty that we saw in the heavens and in our lives together. The magic of the night made us feel like we were in heaven itself, if only for a moment.

Often the little things we do for each other are the ones that we remember the most; like the times when she would do small, loving gestures for me. Once she made a trail of red roses for me to our bedroom and waited as I came in the door from work.

I was at once struck at the sight and felt that warm feeling one gets when your heart is touched with a reminder of the love that is given to you.

Slowly I followed the trail upstairs to our bedroom to find her there grinning with the knowledge that she had touched my heart.

But there were other things, like when she cooked for me or when I brought her breakfast in bed or simply the loving smiles we would exchange whenever we were together.

Stefan would wait up for me when I came home late from work at the fitness center or when I was working on a movie set or rehearsing on a stage. She was there for me.

When I began making my film, *Spiritual Warfare*, she was a part of it, helping in any way that I needed her to; she was there every step of the way. She helped with lighting, booms, and other behind the scenes matters.

Ironically, her role in the movie was that of a dead woman under a sheet in one scene.

Every day I would tell her how beautiful she was and how much I loved her. She was my best friend.

And that love extended to her family as well. Her mother, Paula, was wonderful to me and I felt very close to her.

That probably strikes you as odd, given the fact that I stabbed her 14 times that fateful night; but I never hated her nor had any reason to even dislike her. She was the unfortunate victim of circumstance at the time of what I will call my psychotic break from reality, an apoplectic moment. And that's what I believe it to have been.

What started out as a very bad relationship between Stefan and my mother, finally began to even out after Stefan and I were married and settled down into her apartment. During that short time of our courtship my mother was going after her like a wild animal. She would call her, verbally abuse her and even threaten her if she didn't leave me alone.

My mother, I guess, was projecting her own disappointment in life of not being able to follow her own singing career to its fulfillment onto my life's ambition to become a famous actor. She saw that a relationship and possible marriage would put an end to any hope I may have of becoming a big-name actor. And she was determined to see that nothing stood in the way of that dream – at any cost.

Oddly, she was probably right, but like many 'stage mothers' she took it too far. Perhaps her unrealized dreams were not the same as mine. Oh, I did want to become a big-time actor and filmmaker, but I also wanted a wife and a family; and I believed that both could be possible.

As the voices and the images faded back in to my reality, my head swam with all those past ghosts that will forever haunt me. For days and then weeks the trial trudged forward to its inevitable conclusion.

*　　　*　　　*

The Good Times

Life for me had many good moments; not everything was bad. In fact, part of the reason I have survived so far is because of these good memories of the past.

Not only were there good memories during my time with Stefan (when we met through most of our marriage), but the good memories go back as far as I can recall; from a very early age – around four years old, in fact.

Let me go back to that time; a time with my mother, father, sister, aunts and uncles and the patrons of my dad's restaurant. I was four and the year was 1970.

When I was a little boy, I loved to do skits for my family and friends. I guess, it was my way of escaping the real world that had been cruel in so many ways to me so far.

I would play a variety of different and exotic characters in my little skits; sometimes I would be a brave warrior fighting a flame-breathing monster with a sword, or sometimes only my bare hands. Of course, no matter how ferocious the battle I would always come out on top. Then I would take my bow and smile at the audience.

Other times I would play crazy people; just act goofy and silly. You know, just to get some laughs. If it made them happy and laugh out loud, it gave me pleasure. I was an actor after all.

Still other times I would play characters I have seen on television and at the movie theater, such as cowboys, gangsters and a multitude of others. I would fight Indians, shoot mob leaders and make the world safe again for my folks and others.

I knew then that this was the life for me. Being an actor was the only thing I could ever be. Looking back now I believe that those performances made me feel whole, like this was what I was born to do.

I could see tears of laughter running down their cheeks as they laughed and pointed at what I was doing. That pleasure they displayed and that I felt as well, took me out of my reality and created a safe and happy place that I would return to every time I performed. And it's what keeps me going even now.

That, and working out, both are a form of escape for me. Both are in the moment. Both require complete concentration and dedication to a task. I think that everyone has (or should have) a kind of escape activity from their real existence. No matter how lucky or unlucky in life you may be, we all need some form of escape; that's what entertainment is. That is also what participating in sports is. I, like many others, chose a career (in fact two) that allowed me to escape into the moment much of the time. It was the real world that haunted me; tortured me.

I loved doing plays as I got a little older; always studying famous actors and how they performed. I'd watch the way they talked, moved, showed expression and emotion. Every little part of what made them become real to an audience was important to me. As I mentioned, I took classes at one acting school just to learn how to fall, run into walls, and other kinds of stunts you might see in any action movie. In fact, I would amuse and bewilder my friends at school by running into a wall and falling down like I was injured, only to jump up laughing and without a bump or bruise on me.

These kinds of skills translated well into some of the sports that I participated in during middle and high school.

I played a variety of sports from football and baseball to volleyball and wrestling. During that time, I also worked out with weights and exercised. I became obsessive with doing pushups and can (to this day at 51 years old) do 1,000! I needed to be strong, physically, so that no one could ever abuse me again. Sadly, physically (including sexual) abuse is not the only kind of abuse. What I didn't prepare for was emotional and psychological abuse. Even though I had experienced it during the sexual and physical abuse I had gotten, this kind of abuse is very subtle; and much deadlier.

But the exercise made me feel good, just like performing. They are both a form of therapy for me. While I still work at both, even these past 20 years in prison, it's truly been God's amazing grace, love and forgiveness that has kept me alive throughout this journey in life. Even when it's been hard to forgive myself or others who have hurt and betrayed me, I find refuge in God's grace, and hope in his love.

Much of what I have done as an adult outside in the world was focused on those two sides of my life: exercise and acting. I got a job at *Riverside Fitness Center* while taking any acting job I could to develop my craft. Despite what I had come through, I had made it alive and it looked very promising for me in my future.

I was meeting some good and successful people in the gym and on the stage or set as well. Many of the people that I worked with at the fitness center became social friends of mine. Lawyers, police, other actors; people from all walks of life. Some of them were very interesting and accomplished. The same was true on the theater stage. I acted in *Tony and Tina's Wedding* with a 16-year-old girl named Alecia Beth Moore, who became known as 'Pink' (the famous singer), and on movie sets with many well-known actors and actresses, such as Bruce Willis, Sylvester Stallone and Michelle Pfeiffer, to name a few.

Most of my roles in movies were extra parts or small bit parts where I may have had a line or two, or not. A few I had bigger parts in, but that was more in my future.

In addition to the fitness center and a busy acting career, I was making my own horror films. I first made *Gruesome's Legend* in which I played Tony Gruesome, and then I began work on two others, *Horrorscope* and *Heavenbound*, which Larry Kirschner (who worked almost miracles on the film as I was incarcerated before it was completed) morphed into *Spiritual Warfare*. That film is out on Vimeo at present, while we're working on *Gruesome's Legend* to be released.

But those were the good and (once again) bad times. You might say that both the good and the bad came back into my life in the form of Stefan Broude. It was good and bad, not because of her, but because I believe now that neither one of us were ready for this relationship that was about to begin.

It's true that we make our own happiness. I guess I never knew it at the time, but have learned it over these past 20 years. Twenty years in prison gives one a lot of time to think about a great many things. As I have reflected over the years and observed others around me, I find that my life was a constant barrage of calmness and chaos, one constantly rolling into the other and back again.

In some ways, I became numb to reality. It was then that I could escape into my fantasy world. In other ways, I was a captive of the harsh reality that surrounded me.

We all have fears, usually unrealistic fears, as children; things that make us run and hide under our blankets at night or grab onto our parents' pant-leg hiding our faces from the monsters that are trying to get us. Mine and Michelle's were real; they were real monsters – the people that my parents trusted to take care of us.

Monsters, I could take care of. I did it as young as four when I performed for my relatives, slaying dragons. That was no big deal for me, but the teenage girls, adult men and others that abused us, they were the monsters we couldn't overcome.

It's difficult to relate my life experience without jumping from good to bad because that is how it has played out so far; or I should say up until my incarceration. Since then, life has settled into more of a flow than the extreme highs and lows of the past. Oh, there are plenty of bad times: seeing brothers die in prison, others getting out only to return a short time later, and more. The good often involves the spirituality of many of the men that I live with here at Graterford.

Additionally, I still have my family and some of my good friends from before. I also have a few new friends on the outside that are there for me as well. There is a lot to be grateful for in this life, no matter what your circumstances; that's how I've come to look at it. If my only way to the outside world again is feet first, then I had better make the most of the time God has given me – no matter where I am; because this is all God's domain.

Raised a Roman Catholic, I now profess my faith as a Christian, no longer affiliating myself with the Catholic Church.

I still pray daily as well as read from the scriptures. But as strong as my belief in the Lord, Jesus Christ is, I feel the constant tug from the other side of eternity; that of the Devil.

I have stated more than once that I know that evil exists within and without. I believe the Devil is real and looks for weakness in our faith to lead us into the evils that exist all around us in our daily lives.

I recount the many times I have seen the face of evil in my life and how I have succumbed to these callings.

* * *

10

Photos & Documents

The following photos depict different stages in Stromberg's life & career. The documents relate to the aftermath of the murders.

Top: Larry Stromberg ages 15-50 [1981-2016].
Middle: Stromberg as Tony Gruesome; Stromberg & sister, Michelle
Kraisman, from "Gruesome's Legend" [both 1987].
Bottom: (wife) Stefan Stromberg working on set of "Spiritual Warfare"
[1995] & at aquarium [1994].

101

Top: Stromberg with friend, Charles "Skip" Dougherty, from Stromberg film, "Spiritual Warfare" [1995]; Philadelphia News article [1997].
Middle: Promotional Flyers for "Gruesome's Legend" & "Spiritual Warfare."
Bottom: 2016 photo of Stromberg's mother, Diane; family photo of Diane with brother, Nick, sister, Ramona & granddaughter, Amber, in South Carolina (2017).

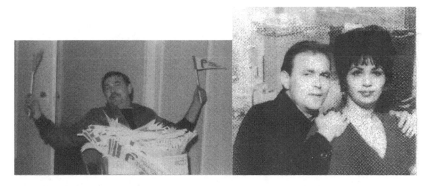

Above left: Larry Sr. after the Phillies won the 1980 World Series;
Above right: Larry Sr. and Diane (taken in the 1970s).

Above left: Cover on one of the tabloids following the murders;
Above right: Stromberg being taken to CFCF (Curran-Fromhold
Correctional Facility) after his arraignment.

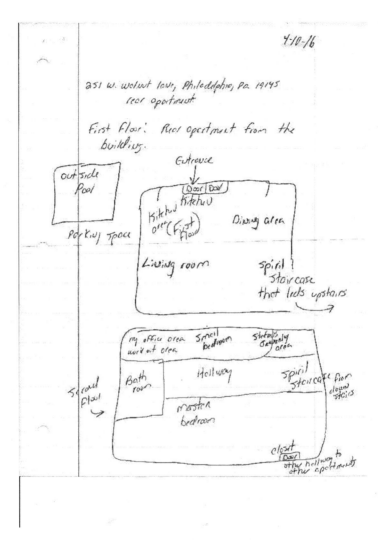

Stromberg's floor plan drawing of the apartment at 251 West Walnut Lane in Germantown (Philadelphia, PA). The murders took place on the first floor at the back of the building in the kitchen.

Letter Stromberg wrote to his lawyer, Nino Tinari, November 12, 2008 concerning a plea bargain that was offered, that Tinari never related to him.

Dear Nino, Nov 12th, 2008

I hope and pray you and ▓▓▓▓ are doing well. We are rehearsing our christmas play. I seen your daughter ▓▓▓▓ in philadelphia magazine and she looks awesome and I know your proud of her. There is a question I need to ask you. Im investigating to seek reinstatement of my appellate rights. Was there any plea offer agreements made by the Commonwealth in my case? Maybe third degree that I didnt know about. Any numbers? Please let me know. →

31   9-7-12

It would be helpful. Thank you and God. bless you and ▓▓▓▓ always.

Sincerly yours
Gary Stromberg

Case 2:09-cv-0040\-CMR Document 42-2 Filed 09/26/   . Page 8 of 62

NINO V. TINARI
ATTORNEY AT LAW

November 20, 2008

Mr. Larry Stromberg
No. D6-6377

Re: <u>Commonwealth vs. Larry Stromberg</u>

Dear Mr. Stromberg:

I received your letter dated November 17, 2008. Thank you for those kind words regarding ████ and you are correct yes, she was awesome and is awesome.

I am not sure what the offer was but I think you are correct it was 40 – 80 years.

Thank you for your kind considerations.

Very Truly Yours,

Nino V. Tinari

9-26-11

***Tinari's November 20, 2008 response to Stromberg, affirming
that there was a plea bargain offered.***

106

11

Jealousy, Rage & Murder

And we made Love almost every night. But Love-making soon became Sex; and Sex became Frustration. Frustration gave way to Desperation; and Desperation soon turned into Loneliness. Loneliness became Apoplexy!

With a mother who told him from the beginning of the relationship that Stefan was no good; that she was a slut – and many other things, Stromberg wasn't confused about whether she was cheating on him. In his mind, he was confused about who she was cheating with and how many men she was sleeping with during that short marriage.

He believed an old boyfriend who was still around was having an affair with her. He was convinced that several men he called friend from the fitness center were sleeping with her. And he was certain she was carrying on with a cook at the restaurant downtown where she had a part-time job.

The uncertainty of not knowing who, when and why led to Stromberg's jealous rages. As he pressed for what he deemed the truth, his rage only grew. Stefan denied any wrongdoing on her part. However, she later admitted to an affair with the cook.

Stromberg began to suspect everyone as they might make a joking remark or advise him to let her go. And those close to him that he didn't suspect – he ignored their advice as well. They all were telling him to leave her and forget about her; that she was no good for him.

Whether she was cheating on him or not, it was a very stormy relationship; much like the one he saw with his parents.

Here, Stromberg tells of the horrors of the brutal deaths of his wife, Stefan Broude Stromberg, and her mother, Paula Rathgeb.

His words convey the rage and pain that were felt that fateful day. They tell of the suffering that all three endured that last evening on earth for two of them and the last evening of freedom for the other.

*   *   *

In His Own Words

When my mother found out about me and Stefan's relationship, she interfered with a fury. She would call Stefan and threaten her; call her a whore. In the end, Stefan said I must choose – her or my mother. I was falling in love with Stefan, so I moved out of my mother's house. I knew I was in love. My heart burned with heartache without her.

I'd go to her apartment, go swimming in the apartment's swimming pool, take a shower with her and start having sex with her every night. She helped me have orgasms. I told her about me being abused as a boy.

I moved into her apartment and that weekend I went to Louisville, Kentucky to meet her father; we got married that weekend. It was the best day of my life.

My mother and father had very different takes on this relationship. My father seemed genuinely happy for us while my mother became depressed and hated my wife with a passion.

I was being pulled in two different directions; trying to make my mother happy while beginning a new life with my new wife, Stefan.

At one point, I moved from our apartment to my parents' house for a few days because of my mother.

I was confused and troubled by all the failed relationships. Stefan had many sexual encounters with men. She was taking psychiatric medication and saw her psychiatrist on a regular basis. She also had trouble with not having orgasms. I knew she was abused in some way; something she was ashamed of. But she never would talk about it with me.

But me and Stefan were happy together.

She, however, didn't feel the same about my mother and once said, "I wish your mother was dead." This made me upset and I acted out in anger and smacked Stefan for saying that.

I started going to therapy.

I began having my own problems. I would work out excessively; rebuke thoughts of suicide. I would not pay attention to my wife's needs.

I suspected she was cheating on me for a long time with other men; some of which I knew and thought of as friends.

Stefan left to go to Florida to visit her mother and to have an abortion. The baby was either mine or the Asian cook's from *Long's Gourmet Chinese Restaurant*, where Stefan worked part-time.

Why didn't I leave her? Well, from being sexually abused beyond measure as a boy and being a virgin when I met her and had intercourse, I couldn't walk away. With my own mental issues and being bi-polar I wouldn't walk away from her. I chose to forgive her and try to work things out with her. Many called me a fool.

We made love almost every night. But then it stopped. I became obsessed to fix my marriage.

Stefan would tell me she loved me and wanted to work things out.

Then she would tell me the opposite. It went back and forth for months. I was slowly going insane. I was hearing voices. It was the voice of the devil. I was praying to God to help me. I was losing my mind.

She would at times have sex with me. It was like a drug to me. It would calm me down, make things feel normal again. But then I would say to myself, "I would miss the abuse, the pain." This made me question my sanity. I couldn't let her go. I wanted to so bad.

Stefan would be jealous when I got acting jobs in films, plays and acting with beautiful women.

We both had our own sexual addictions.

I was hearing voices in my head to do horrible things; to kill all the men who were sleeping with my wife and then to kill her to end all the pain in my heart.

I would rebuke that evil voice in the name of Jesus Christ.

I could feel the frustration; and this time a full scale demonic attack was coming on me.

This went on for weeks. I became even more obsessive. Stefan was still working at the restaurant where one of her lovers was a cook.

She was still seeing other men including her old boyfriend, Bob.

I had had enough. On a Sunday in March of 1996 I went to work and told Stefan I would be home at 1:00 p.m. When I got there, she was gone. I waited for three hours, having a panic attack, when she walked in with Bob.

She said they walked the dogs and then went to lunch.

She told me she wanted me to move out and that we could be friends.

She couldn't take me buying her things anymore; that I walked around like a hurt puppy.

I begged her again. She got up and said I'm out of here. I told her we're gonna talk this out. I went to the door first and wouldn't let her leave. I asked her, "Did you screw Bob today?"

She reached into the cabinet drawer and pulled out a knife and raised it at me. I said, "It's come to this, huh?". I grabbed the knife from her and I put on a pair of white gloves and picked her up on my shoulders and carried her into the bedroom. I placed her on the bed. It was like I was controlled by an evil force. I placed my hands around her neck and started to choke her. Then I backed

111

off. I stood above her and told her I'm sorry and then I started to remove her clothes. She said, "No!".

I couldn't stop. I had to feel intimacy with her. I had to make love to her like in days' past when we were so happy. So, I forced myself on her. Then slowly she agreed and we were making love. It was wrong how this happened. This is not what God wanted me to do. I told her, over and over again, I was sorry.

The next day we went to a therapist named Bryan Cohen, who I was in counseling with. Stefan was in therapy with Dr. Sandy Cohen, his mother. We told him what happened. He said we were in a downslide if we didn't get help. That I should take medication to calm down my anxiety attacks; that we should be in therapy as a couple.

We rented a movie, went home and made love. Stefan told me she loved me and that we were gonna work things out. Every time I made love to Stefan it was magical to me. It also relieved the pain in my heart caused by her adultery.

I could forgive her if she would be loyal to me and be my faithful wife once again.

We would go to see a Broadway show, to the art museum, go out to dinner. We had a great time.

I was getting good acting jobs that paid big money, such as a training video for the Pennsylvania police that paid five grand for just three days' work. Things were looking hopeful for us.

But that wouldn't last long. She was still cheating on me. Renting hotel rooms at her lunch break to see the coworker from Long's restaurant and another lover, a mutual friend of ours.

The next thing I knew she packed a suitcase when her stepsister and the stepsister's daughter were staying with us.

Just days before Stefan talked me into filing for bankruptcy with her because of excessive credit card debt from all the jewelry she bought for her business and my film supplies while making *Spiritual Warfare.*

I was stupid to agree. My mother told me not to do it. It's like I did anything she asked just to keep her with me.

She packed and got in her truck and left.

I called her at the restaurant and said I was coming there to see her.

Three of my friends, Sean along with Pete and Brad (not their real names) came to the apartment to make sure I stayed away from the restaurant. Stefan stayed in a hotel room with her mother who came up from Florida.

Stefan's stepfather, Neill (Rathgeb), called me and threatened me. I changed the locks on the apartment the next day.

A week went by and I decided to go down to the restaurant. I walked in and all eyes were on me like I was an evil person. Her eyes looked like she was happy to see me. We went outside to talk. I asked her to come back home with me and be my faithful wife. The cook came outside to check on her.

I told her I would be at Bryan Cohen's tomorrow for therapy.

The next day, in the morning, I went to the therapy session. After a few minutes, Stefan came into the room in a fury. She told me she wanted me out of her life; out of the apartment. I agreed. I asked her to give me a few days to move. She said yes and left.

I figured now it was over. I was beginning to accept that. I left Bryan's house, rented a U-Haul truck, and found an apartment to move into.

My mom and sister were at the apartment as I was getting boxes to move. My friend Pete and I went to the house, but my mother and sister told me I couldn't go in because Stefan and Paula were in there and Stefan had filed a restraining order against me for rape. I had to wait for the police to come to get some things out of the house with Spartagus and Bandit, my dogs.

We left to go pick up my dad from work at a Jazz Restaurant where he made the best pizza in town.

I told my mom and Michelle to watch the dogs. I went around the corner and into a strip club. I paid a woman to have sex with me.

She said, "If I was your wife I would never cheat on you." She told me I was beautiful. Of course, I paid her and she was gonna say what I wanted to hear.

I thanked her and left the room and the club called *Les Girls*. It no longer exists.

I went back to my dad's workplace and then we all went to their house in Lancaster.

Since I couldn't be at the apartment on West Walnut when Stefan was there, my family and friends moved my things out and into my new apartment on Elmwood Avenue in Belmont Hills.

A few days later I had to be at a hearing in family court in Philadelphia to agree to stay away from Stefan for a year.

A part of me was relieved. I didn't have to live in the hellish situation anymore.

I was planning on editing my film *Spiritual Warfare* and maybe start dating different women.

I started praying for God to help me. But I did sense an evil presence trying to destroy me, telling me, "Your adulteress wife wants to have sex with others now that your gone."

I said to myself, "It's time to let go; to move on. She doesn't love you. Trust God now."

I saw Sean at the fitness center and he said, "She's with the Asian lover. She's taking it all in, Stromberg." This really pissed me off.

My mind was in a stir of madness. Was Stefan having sex with the co-worker at the apartment tonight?

I left my new apartment and walked the eight miles to my old apartment to see if this was true.

I arrived at the apartment on West Walnut after midnight. It was dark. Stefan's truck was there. I tried to climb up to the window.

Stefan and her mother turned the lights on. I knocked on the door and heard Paula yell out, "Who's there?" I decided to leave before the police came. I walked back to my apartment saying to myself, "I'm done."

It was like something was controlling me; like I was possessed in some way. The devil was using my pain, my past, other people to kill me; to put crazy thoughts in my head.

All the terrible things from my past and present were surrounding me: a controlling mother, a passive father, a drug addicted, suicidal sister, sexual and physical abuse as a child, Stefan's affairs. All these were spinning around me now.

When I went back to my apartment I still prayed that Stefan and I would find a way to work it out. I remembered all the wonderful times we had together at the Jersey Shore, our wedding day, our trip to Florida, walking hand in hand in the park and more.

But then I thought of the affairs she had and it crushed the good memories and sent me into a depressed, empty state of mind.

Shortly after this my mother gave me a letter Stefan gave her the day they moved me out. Stefan also gave her a braided cross necklace she made for me.

In the letter, Stefan said that, "Our wedding day was the happiest day of my life and I never loved anybody how I loved you."

Reading this touched me and it also brought on heartache. I walked Spartagus and Bandit and then lay on the floor of my apartment next to them. It was as if they knew my pain. They stayed by my side all night to comfort me.

The next morning at 10:00 a.m. I had to be in family court. As I waited in the lobby, Stefan and her lawyer came in; she turned back at me and smiled. She looked beautiful; my heart dropped. Her lawyer approached me and told me the procedure. I entered the courtroom and agreed to the restraining abuse protection order to stay away from Stefan.

I went to work on an *HBO* movie at the Philadelphia airport that evening and met an actress named Rita (not her real name) that I knew. She was a beautiful woman. We made plans to see each other. I told her I would call her tomorrow.

I left the airport and headed to the train station to go home. As I walked on Market Street in Center City the temptation hit me as I walked past *Les Girls*. I stopped and entered the club, paying a Spanish stripper to have sex with me. As I reached my climax I felt a sense of death; the effects of sin, the tailspin of madness and darkness that was consuming my soul, mind, body and spirit.

I longed for peace.

By the time I got back to my apartment it was 3:00 in the morning. I walked my dogs, knowing I had to be at the fitness center at 8:00 a.m.

For the short time I had to finally rest, I fell away on the floor, again with my dogs, and dreamed about falling into an abyss. I was falling and falling into darkness when a hand reached down and pulled me up. It was the hand of Jesus Christ. I looked right into his eyes of compassion.

I woke up out of the dream knowing that it was real.

I knew then that I could make it without Stefan. It was time for a new start. I felt content and asked the good Lord to forgive me of my sins.

When I went to work that morning at the fitness center Sean came in and told me that Stefan was going to call me and he said not to take her call. I stayed calm and stayed away from him after that.

Not too long after, the gym's manager buzzed me and told me that I had a phone call, and it was from my ex. He asked if I wanted to take it.

I hesitated, knowing that I longed to talk to her. I took the call.

When I heard her voice, it brought complete joy to my heart, my soul.

She asked, "Are you mad at me, Larry?"

I replied, "No."

I told her that I loved her, and she told me that she loved me too. She asked me where I was last night and told me that she tried to reach me at my apartment. She said she called there over 40 times!

117

MJ Maccalupo

I reminded her of the restraining order and that I didn't want to go to jail. She replied that she didn't want me to go to jail either.

Ironically, one of the things he was charged with at trial was Contempt of Court for violating this court order.

She asked me again where I was last night. I told her about the movie shoot, but not about Rita or the stripper.

I must admit I enjoyed hearing her ask where I was last night. We talked and decided to meet at one that afternoon at the bridge by Main Street in Manayunk. I was so excited; I was walking in a cloud, hoping to work things out and make love to her. So, I waited until 12:30 and checked out of work.

That would be the last day I worked at *Riverside Fitness* after seven years of employment there.

When I got to the bridge Stefan's truck pulled up and I got in. I asked her if she wanted to go to lunch and she replied, "No. Take me to your apartment."

We went there and took Spartagus and Bandit for a walk like we used to. She was happy to see them, and they were happy to see her again as well.

Stefan told me that she was going to drop the restraining order and that I should have never raped her. She told me that it would kill her to see me with another woman when I win an award for acting or filmmaking.

She told me that she had never met anyone like me before. She asked that we agree not to see other people and to go to therapy together.

She remarked, "I wished that I would have met you five years later when you were more mature. Why did I have to meet you?"

She said that she now believed in God. I asked her to make love and she said not yet.

In my confused state of mind, I desperately wanted to make love to her, to connect with her once again. I was out of control and forced myself on her.

She said, "I trusted you." But I just wanted, I needed, to feel her love like I did during our happy times together.

It was a crazy lust burning in my head. Why did I rape her again? Why?

Was I an evil person; just a selfish person trying to find a sense of control? Did I want to just hurt her for hurting me? Was I becoming self-destructive? Did an evil spirit control me?

As I slowly let Stefan go, she said that she would call me; I knew that that was a lie. She said, "We need to get you help, Larry."

I told her we were abusing each other and she responded, "Yes, we are."

I walked her to her truck and looked her in her eyes. I knew that this would be goodbye for good.

She drove off.

I lay back down on the floor that evening with my two dogs and fell into a deep sleep.

I missed work the next morning and didn't even answer the phone when it rang, or the door when someone began knocking.

After a great deal of persistent knocking, I finally opened the door and my friend Gary (not his real name) was there. He was one of the people that I trained at the center on Sunday mornings. He told me that they were worried about me when I didn't show. He told me that I should let Stefan go; that she was no good for me. I knew he was right, but I was possessed by something that wouldn't let me let go.

I left the apartment and walked to the local *Wawa Convenience Store*. There I bought myself a turkey hoagie and an iced tea. I stood in the cashier's line waiting to pay when this strange man who was standing in line next to me asked, "You want a ride to downtown Philly? You're an actor, huh?".

I said, "I am."

He said, "I'm not a strange person. I'll drive you downtown."

He told me he was from L.A. and that he was an actor. He said, "We all are actors in this thing called life."

So, I got in his car. On the way, he stopped to buy a case of beer and then drove me down I-95 to Center City, Philadelphia. We drove by *Eastern State Penitentiary*, which closed in the 1960s, and he said, "Be careful; you could be in a prison like that with Bubba."

He told me, "Your wife is a sexual person and so are you, Larry."

How did this person who I never met in my life know this about me? He pulled up to the rehearsal location and said, "This is your stop, huh?".

I said, "Thank you," and got out of his car.

He added, "You need God's help, Larry."

I walked away wondering if this was a message from God; was this guy an angel or something?

After the rehearsal, my friend Pete picked me up and drove us back to my apartment.

He said, "I thought there would be a murder-suicide at your apartment. Why are you so screwed up over her?".

I related my past sexual abuse and evil thoughts of revenge to him.

He smiled and said, "Success is the best revenge. Go out and date other women; work on your career."

I walked the dogs and checked my phone messages. Stefan didn't call; Rita did. Then my friend Ted (not his real name) called and said, "You'll get over Stefan. Don't have sex with her."

I thought that odd and wondered, "Why would he say that?".

*   *   *

12

Decent into Madness

April 28, 1996

It was a time out of control. Jealousy turned to rage, and the flames of rage were fanned by the voices he heard.

My mother called to make sure I was okay.

I sat there in the apartment in a quiet trance, alone with my thoughts; thoughts of Stefan having sex with other men. Thinking all kinds of crazy things.

This is when I believe full possession of my soul by the devil took place.

It comes first from *infestation*, then *oppression* and then *possession*.

You see, the devil and his demons seek out a person for a purpose. Scripture clearly states this fact.

Be sober, be vigilant; because your adversary the devil, as a roaring lion, walketh about, seeking whom he may devour. 1 Peter 5:8

At this point in my life I had backed away from God; from my personal relationship with Christ. I was making horror films, having sex with strippers, fixating over my wife; I was dealing with severe mental illness.

For jealousy is the rage of a man; therefore, he will not spare in the day of vengeance. Proverbs 6:34

The devil loves to infest those who were abused. He thrives on their violated ways; their damaged souls; their innocence lost. That's when the devil will find the opportune time to start the *infestation* of a person's soul; of my soul.

The *oppression* was coming down on me to destroy me; to commit suicide and end it all. I was a failure; I wanted to die.

I sat down, falling into a state of *possession*. Something was in control of me in full force. I sat there listening to rock and roll and a song came on the radio called, *Now You're Messing with a Son-of-a-Bitch*, by the band Nazareth.

I got up, packed my backpack with two swords, a nightstick, a ski mask and a bible (small bible for Stefan). I put my knife in my pocket. I was going to the restaurant to kill Stefan, to kill her lovers.

Then, I would die.

I said goodbye to Spartagus and Bandit and left my apartment.

I walked down Main Street in Manayunk on a suicide mission. When I arrived at the bus station I stopped and something told me to go to my old apartment on West Walnut Lane in Germantown.

So, I waited for the 65 bus. When it arrived, I got on and at that point my mind was in a trance. The bus was full of people, their faces all looking at me.

In my mind, I would find Stefan with one of her lovers at the apartment. The bus ride seemed long and slow. A chill was running through my body; my heart was pounding.

As the bus turned onto the street I saw the 1995 black Ford Ranger that belonged to Stefan in the parking lot of the apartment house.

I got off at the stop by the rear apartment at 251 West Walnut and Green Lane.

At the corner of those streets is a large church. I slowly looked around as I stood on the sidewalk and then decided to walk down Green Lane and make a left into a driveway. The driveway led to the back entrance of the apartment.

I walked to the back entrance. I saw Stefan and her mother with Mildred Lilly, a neighbor who also lived in the old mansion that had been converted into apartments.

They were packing things up and this sent me into a panic; a frenzy of delusion. I was scared; out of my mind. My mind was flashing thoughts of abandonment; something psychotic. My mind snapped.

I tried to fight this evil spirit speaking to me to kill. All my subconscious feelings and conflicts began to surface. I walked away from the huge wooden fence and told myself to leave. A force pulled me back to the fence. And each time I resisted by walking away. And each time I walked away the voice called me back.

As I stood behind the wooden fence, I saw Paula speaking on a phone to someone. I assumed it was her husband Neill Rathgeb, who was in Florida where they lived.

I looked at the apartment and saw Lilly talking to Stefan, getting ready to leave to go to her own apartment. I saw Stefan giving Lilly things, as if she was moving out, leaving.

I didn't notice, but when Lilly left she went over to a clothesline to take in a rug she had hung up earlier.

The front door was wide open from when Stefan and her mother, Paula, walked Lilly outside to say goodbye. No one had observed me as I paced back and forth in my black clothing hidden by the darkness and surrounding bushes and fence.

I stood there as I was torn by voices telling me to: "Go in," "Don't go in," "Leave," "Kill," "Run," "Do it!".

The devil and his demons had control of me. I heard a voice speak to me, saying, "Now, it's time!" Eerily, this was a line from my film, *Gruesome's Legend*. Now I repeated it out loud, "Now, it's time!" Loud enough so that Lilly heard me.

A force moved me. It called me to run into the apartment like a maniac, a madman.

I ran across the lawn hunched over moving at a very fast speed. I rushed into the apartment and entered the wide-open front door with the knife in my left hand.

Stefan and Paula were standing in the kitchen.

This is very hard to talk about, as I can't believe I did what I did. I loved these two people; my wife and my mother-in-law.

I quickly entered the apartment seeing everything in black and white. It was as if I was floating above the turmoil, watching

125

as I swung my knife at these two women. Stefan screamed. Paula moved towards me and said, "You're sick, Larry!".

It was like my spirit had left my body. It was as if I was looking down on this horrible evil act. I had no control over my movements; my body was controlled by the devil.

I pushed Paula to the ground. She fell to the floor face first. I stabbed her in the back and could hear the knife going through her body and hit the floor. I will never forget that horrific sound, nor the sounds of Paula and Stefan as their screams echoed throughout the apartment in a chilling way.

Stefan just stood there screaming as I rushed towards her and began stabbing away repeatedly in an uncontrollable fashion.

Her screams got louder and louder as I stabbed her, hitting her body and face. Paula hit me on the back with a broom. I turned towards her, pushing her back onto the ground, and stabbed her again and again.

It may sound odd, but Paula was the bravest woman I would ever know.

Paula lay on the ground as Stefan continued to stand. I turned back to Stefan and began to stab her over and over again, in the chest, in the face and in the eye.

I heard her say, "I'm over." Then, she fell to the floor, losing control of her body.

I stood there for a short moment in a different world. What I had done was from the depths of Hell.

I heard police sirens in the distance that became louder and louder. It was reality setting back in.

I ran out the front of the apartment crouching down, the same as I had entered. I ran fast, like a wild animal.

Stefan's and Paula's screams were silenced, but play back in my head to this day. I pray that one day I will see them in Heaven.

And God shall wipe away all tears from their eyes; and there shall be no more death, neither sorrow, nor crying, neither shall there be any more pain; for the former things are passed away. Revelation 21:4

As I ran through the backyard of the apartment it felt surreal, strange; like the end of days.

I climbed over a fence and threw the knife and backpack away into a dumpster.

The police sirens were roaring louder and louder as I ran across the street and saw a group of young African-American male teenagers sitting on the front porch of a house, talking. I walked up to them and asked to use their cell phone.

They looked at me with fear in their eyes, like I was insane, as I gave them my mother and father's phone number. They dialed the phone number. My mother answered and I said, "Mom, I think I killed Stefan and Paula. Please go get Spartagus and Bandit from my apartment."

My mother screamed out, "No Larry!".

I said, "Please get my dogs and take them to your house. I love you. I'll call you again soon."

I hung up the phone and thanked the young men. I walked away fast. They looked at me like I was a crazy, insane man. That day I was.

127

As I walked quickly away I could hear the police sirens getting louder and louder still.

I looked for a place to rest. I climbed over another fence into a secured location. It was the gloom all around me that laid a blanket of despair over my eyes and head as I entered the yard of the dark estate.

A large brown pit bull was standing in front of me; he growled. I bent down and the dog walked over to me, smelling me. I hugged him. I believe God sent me to that dog to be comforted by him. As I hugged him, I slowly came back to myself. I fell to my knees knowing Satan had me in his grip; controlling me to commit this horrible act of evil.

He used everything in my life that was evil for this moment of murder: the sexual abuse, my psychological disorders, the horror films I wrote and acted in. I became those vile characters I created: Tony Gruesome from *Gruesome's Legend*, Von Kraven and Eddie Kraven from *Spiritual Warfare* all driven by hate, anger and revenge.

Stefan's infidelity, her tormenting me by sexually starving me at her whim and then taking the pain away only to find a new way to torture my soul. I felt like I was killing the sexual predators that raped me over 100 times as a boy. I wanted revenge for the violation I felt. I wanted to kill the men she was having sex with. I wanted the pain to end; I wanted my life to end.

My life was over. I destroyed many lives that night. I sat crying for everyone I hurt. Death would be the best thing for me.

I saw shadows, dark ones move around me, demons wanting me to take my life and complete the devil's final goal for me.

I sat contemplating suicide.

As I walked out of the estate I came to a high bridge. A hundred feet below I could see cement. I stood there about to jump off when I heard a voice, the voice of the Holy Spirit perhaps, speaking to me, telling me to live.

When I heard this, I turned and walked away into the unknown.

I arrived at a bus stop and got on a Septa (Southeastern Pennsylvania Transit Authority) bus traveling to Chestnut Hill. I went into the *Borders Bookstore* to use the restroom to get cleaned up. I saw blood on my sneakers and pant legs. I washed it off as best I could and went to the food counter to get something to drink and eat.

I left the bookstore and found an empty shed to sleep in for the next two days. It rained those days. The rain poured down as if it were the angels crying. I slept as the night ended in the morning and then into the afternoon and once again into night. After at least 24 hours I stepped out to face the unknown.

I next walked up Germantown Pike Road and found a parking lot with empty school buses. I stopped at a pizza shop, bought a pizza and soda and sat in an empty school bus and enjoyed one of my last meal out in society. I slept there that night.

When I moved on, I stopped at a church and looked at the statues. As I sat in the church in deep thought, in deep prayer, the statues seemed to be moving and watching me as I got up and walked through the church. They began to speak to me. I had to leave.

The rain started; a cold rain. I found a dry place inside a large cardboard box by a trash dumpster.

After this I walked up the street to a restaurant on Germantown Pike where I saw people that I knew from the fitness center sitting in a booth. They looked at me with eyes wide open. I felt as if they knew and were uneasy eating with a man on the run.

I ate my food, used the restroom and washed up. I then called a friend to contact my mother and father to let them know that I was still alive. I left the restaurant as quickly as possible.

I then walked to a *Wawa Convenience Store* to buy a newspaper. I was on the front cover.

I purchased the paper as a state police officer entered the store and looked at me, then looked away and bought a coffee.

I went outside and used a payphone to make another phone call. I called a friend and told him to call my mother and father for someone to pick me up and to arrange my surrender. I told him my location at Miles Park.

He told me, "Neil Abrams will pick you up."

I thanked him and hung up the phone. I walked over to the school and waited.

As I sat waiting, I read the article in the paper about me; the murders, my life, acting career, my marriage problems and being on the run. Then a silver Lexus pulled into the parking lot. It was Abrams. I got into the car. He seemed scared and nervous. When he arrived (he later told reporters in a television interview) I was rolling on the ground, dirty, unshaven and incoherently rambling to myself. I have no recollection of this.

We drove to his house and he told me Stefan and Paula were dead. Everyone thought I had committed suicide.

I took a shower and placed the bloody clothes in a large bag. I called my mother and father while Abrams arranged my surrender by calling a friend of his in the FBI.

We had to be at the roundhouse police station at 3:00 a.m.

As we drove down I-95 to Center City, Philadelphia it seemed surreal; mystic in a way. It would be my last night out in society.

When we entered the police station Detective Danks stopped me and I handed him the paper bag containing the bloody clothes I was wearing during the murders. I gave him a full confession without the presence of a lawyer. I was ready to die. Nothing mattered anymore. They processed me, took mug shots and fingerprints.

I was then sent to another police station near the art museum on Hamilton Street; the same street where *Long's Chinese Restaurant* was located; the place Stefan had worked part-time.

I fell asleep and was awakened by Sean, my friend who was a captain on the Philadelphia Police Force. He told me he understood me killing Stefan, but not the mother.

I was so tired and out of touch with reality that I didn't care what happened to me.

Sean, my friend for seven years, the man I played basketball with, went to powerlifting contests with, a man whose wife and daughter I knew, handcuffed me and shackled my ankles.

He told me I would be able to buy a television when I went upstate and that there were news people awaiting me.

That was the last time I saw Sean.

131

As the police walked me outside, the news reporters and cameras were everywhere.

Their question, "Larry, why did you do it?".

I had no comment. I didn't know why I did it. Why would I hurt and kill Stefan and Paula? Why would I destroy my life? I was never in trouble in my life. Now, I'm a murderer.

I was taken to the Philadelphia county jail, sitting in the police van hands cuffed and legs shackled, dreams ended, friends disowned me, my future unknown.

I was headed to prison, the same prison that only a year before I had shot scenes for my film, *Spiritual Warfare* in.

I was processed into CFCF (Curran-Fromhold Correctional Facility), still in a fog. I was put into a cell with 20 other men during the processing where there were bad meals and one toilet.

In prison (initially) I felt a dark hooded figure choking me – waking me in the middle of the night.

The days went on as we would be moved from cell to cell. As I laid on the filthy floor I would hear a voice in my mind. The voice was very clear. It was Stefan's voice saying, "Join me, Larry, join me."

Once I told the prison psychiatrist about the voice, I was escorted to the suicide unit and placed in a single observation cell. I was put on medication as well.

I would sleep and sleep, only to be interrupted by psychiatrist meetings, meals, showers, and day room time where I could call my family.

Next, the lawyers started coming at me. Because this was a high-profile case all the vultures were circling. I was still on the cover of newspapers and tabloids, as well as on television news programs.

Lawyers I knew from *Riverside Fitness* for years all came to represent me. Vladimir Zdrok, Neil Jokelson, Nino Tinari, Calvin Lentz and Russell Axelrod (who I acted with in a play) all wanted the job.

Vladimir Zdrok told me he was offered book and movie deals about my life. The book would be called, "Slasher, the Larry Stromberg Story." He said these would help my case.

He had the television crew from the show *Hard Copy* in the prison, ready to interview me. This was a big mistake, but I was on heavy medication and didn't want to live, so I let him represent me and do the TV interview.

That interview was used against me a year later at my trial. In fact, it was used as the only proof that I wasn't insane at the time of the murderers.

When I went before the judge for the initial hearing I had fired Zdrok and told the judge to just kill me. He ordered me to be evaluated by a psychiatrist to see if I was competent to stand trial.

I then told them to have Neil Jokelson represent me. But that's when Zdrok came in with Nino Tinari and his wife Carol.

Tinari was a big-time criminal defense attorney in the 70s who represented many high-profile clients and had many acquittals.

It was at this time that I was transferred to the detention center on State Road and placed in A-Block with all the other high-profile cases. Homosexuals everywhere; murderers, child molesters, kiddie-porn filmmakers, and rapists were all there. Stabbings and rapes occurred all the time.

My only fight there was with a 300-pound inmate. The guards allowed it. It was something out of the movie *Fight Club*. I won that fight.

*   *   *

13

The Interview – Part 1

On Wednesday, July 13, Jack DiSarno, an associate, and I met with Stromberg at S.C.I. Graterford for approximately five hours. This was my first meeting with him and a very eye-opening one indeed. As I had never been to a prison before, I was amazed at the order and calmness that surrounded us as we met with Stromberg to do an in-depth interview with him.

I can't say the same for DiSarno regarding past experience with prisons. In his former work experience as a County Manager, he had conducted research on county jails and has visited several. He has also visited several state prisons connected to his work and has handed New Testaments to county jail inmates as part of a previous religious affiliation. Despite this, he confessed that he was nervous all day during our time at Graterford.

When we entered the prison, we found ourselves in a large room with lockers on one end, benches set up in rows in front of them and an open area with a raised semi-circular office area. This area had several lines: one was for check in, the other was for sign in.

After checking in and presenting photo ID you signed in at the other station half way around this larger counter area. Following this you sat and waited to be called. In the meantime, you had time to purchase a money card and put all your personal items in a locker to be picked up on your way out.

The 'money card', as I refer to it here is the only 'cash' you can bring with you. You use this to purchase soft drinks, candy bars or chips for yourself and/or the prisoner you are visiting.

After purchasing our card, we sat on one of the long wooden benches watching others being called to meet with their friend or loved one. An officer came out from a room with a clipboard and called off the name of the prisoner to be seen and the visitor got up and followed him into the room. They were called in small groups of maybe five to seven at a time.

"Stromberg…" We heard his last name bellowed out so we got up and moved to the door of the small room that is used to do a search for drugs or any other paraphernalia. We were told to turn our pockets inside out and hold our hands out while they swabbed them with a cotton ball. We then were told to put our hands under a special light that hung on the wall.

"What is this for?" I naïvely asked.

As the two male officers smiled at one another, one responded, "To see if you have any drugs coated on your hands."

A bit embarrassed at my lack of detention knowledge, I further inquired, "Why would anyone have drugs on their hands?"

At this, one of the guards laughed and said, "It's a way to smuggle drugs to the prisoner. The visitor has cocaine or heroin coated on their hands and the prisoner licks it off to get high. You wouldn't believe what some people try to get away with."

We all chuckled.

I awkwardly blurted out, "This is my first time in prison; I mean, the first time I've ever been to one to visit anyone or in one for any reason." I blushed at how foolish I must have appeared, but I'm sure they've heard it before.

We next had to put our belts or anything else we still had into small baskets that lined a long, narrow table in the middle of this small rectangular room.

Then we were told to go around the table and walk through an x-ray machine, much like you would at an airport. They then used a hand wand to further look for contraband.

Since I was carrying a small pad and pen, I was told to put it in the basket with my belt. I told the guard that said this that I had permission from the Superintendent's office to bring this to take notes during our meeting with Stromberg.

The other checked his clipboard and agreed that I had permission.

We were then led to a door that went down a flight of stairs to another door that was on the right of the landing on the bottom. The entire place was concrete, cinder blocks and steel.

The guards stood at the top of the stairs and told us to go through the door at the bottom on the right side and report to the guard station straight ahead.

When we entered, we were in a large room, in what was the basement of the prison. There were similar wooden benches in the area directly in front of us. Seated were men in prison garb waiting for their visitor to arrive.

As I scanned the men I tried to imagine Stromberg, now 20 years older than in the pictures that I had received from his mother, Diane.

My eyes stopped at a middle-aged, balding man and knew that must be him. He looked at us, stood up and smiled as he began to approach. It was Larry Stromberg.

We shook hands and then a hug. It was as if I had known him for years. Up to this point our only means of communication was weekly (sometimes bi-weekly) phone conversations (either 15 or 30 minutes at a time), letters or information conveyed through either Stromberg's uncle Nick or his mother, Diane.

The room was 'T' shaped. The door at the top of the 'T' extended to the guard station (at the intersection of the top and the leg of the 'T') and then to a slightly raised platform, where photos were taken by one of the prisoners. This was for visitors who wanted to purchase the pictures taken with the prisoner they were visiting. The prisoner taking the photos used a small, pink digital automatic camera from which he could download the pictures to a printer and make a 4x6 print to give you before you left. We took some during our visit, one of which is on the cover of this book.

Past the picture area were the snack machines where we later bought some soft drinks and candy bars for the three of us with the money card.

Our first duty was to report to the guard station that sat perched on a stage-like platform, so that the guards could watch everyone in every part of the room.

In front was a long room filled with four rows of wooden benches that stretched for about 25 or 30 feet from the station to

138

two small rooms at the end. One bench ran the length of each cinder block wall with two back-to-back benches running down the middle. This gave maximum visibility to the guards.

The two rooms that sat side-by-side at the very end of this long corridor had plexiglass doors and windows so anyone inside would be visible to the guards, yet allow for quiet conversation without the noise from the other prisoners and their visitors, which included screaming kids running around the room.

We were given one of these rooms by the Sergeant on duty. The other guard asked about my pen and pad, but the Sergeant already knew about it and allowed us to proceed to one of the rooms.

We spent the next five hours in the room talking and praying with Stromberg, praying for guidance in life that we will make good choices and work to help others. Stromberg struck me as a man that truly has found Christ and has learned to live his life for the betterment of others.

In our conversation, it seemed that, while his early years were a mix of chaos, abuse and religious fervor, every part of his life was mimicking reality, not living it. That is, there was a sense that his daily prayer and Bible reading were merely his crying out for help, not understanding that the help lie within him and not from some stranger that would save him. It seemed that he believed his parents would save him, his friends would save him, and even that Stefan would save him. But they all failed because it wasn't their role to save him. He seemed to be at peace with the knowledge that he had to save himself through Jesus Christ so that he could really be freed from the demons that had haunted him for so many years.

*   *   *

Following are the notes from the conversation we had during our visit on July 13, 2016. Questions or comments to Stromberg are italicized. Notes are italicized and in brackets.

The conversation began with some informal introductions and general chit-chat on a range of various topics, after which it sometimes jumped from one topic to another and then landing back again at the original question. In other words, the tone was familiar and conversational, letting Stromberg move the discussion at times as he also had points that he wished to cover.

Tell us about the plays that you have written, and about Lifers, Inc.

Lifers, Inc. already existed when I first went to S.C.I Coal Township, which is where I spent my first 19 years of incarceration, in E-block. It is west of here, more in the middle of the state. Lifers, Inc. is a group of prisoners, as the name implies, that are in for a life sentence. Through this group, I could present my plays to fellow inmates; and in fact, have some of them perform them with me. During that time, we would rehearse every Friday. I had 12 players then, men willing to perform on stage; and believe me, many of them were too shy and had to be given a great deal of encouragement to become a part of the performances. But many of them found that they enjoyed it and even began to really get into the role that they played.

I wrote around 60 plays throughout those years at Coal Township, with the encouragement of many people, including staff members such as Reverends Gail Bryant, Michael Torres, and

Michael Comick (who was recently transferred to Graterford). And there were others as well. Rev. Jane Thomas along with Rev. Comick now work with me at Graterford.

Several of the plays that I have written and had performed are *Running with the Devil*, a play on drug addiction, *Second Chance* and *Life Behind the Razor Wire* about life in prison and the chance to atone for one's crimes.

[*A list of Stromberg's plays, along with his performances on stage and in movies and television, appears in the appendices at the end of the book*]

Besides writing, rehearsing and performing plays, I was encouraged to join a choir by Rev. Gail Bryant. I say encouraged (laughing to himself); what I mean is, she said, 'Mr. Stromberg, I'm going to give you two choices. Either you are going to join the chorus or you're going to become an usher.' I told her I didn't want to do that. She said, 'You have no choice.' Later, she told me, 'Now you're going to write a play.' I said, 'What?' She told me, 'You're going to write a play. You have no choice. Because you're anointed to do so.' The play I wrote is called *The Persecution of Christmas Eve*, which I'm proud of. She directed it.

In January 2015, there was a fire at Northumberland County Prison and so 208 prisoners were moved from there to Coal Township. They were living in the gym for a while. Some of those 208 were sent to S.C.I. Muncy. Because of this fire and shifting of prisoners, some of us at Coal Township were moved to other prisons. The third wave of moves sent me to S.C.I. Graterford where we sit today.

141

At first, I was placed in G-Block, but now I'm in A-Block in a single cell; this is the honor block, which you must earn the right to be moved into.

In the past, I have had all kinds of cellmates; some black, some white, some Hispanic, some gay, and some with a strong faith in God. I got along with all of them.

I do have to admit that I enjoy having a cell to myself now.

I have had various jobs at the two prisons from janitor to food service. Now I work in the staff dining hall, which is a good job; but I never complained about any of them and I always did the best that I could, whatever the job. That probably had something to do with being put into the honor block.

Some of the realities of life in prison would be startling to an outsider. We take showers in groups, but wear sweat shorts while showering, to help prevent rapes from occurring there. But rapes do occur in many different areas of the prison, as do deaths from stabbings, etc.

In prison, a person doesn't even have to rape another person, there's plenty of sex to be had. Sex with other inmates, with female guards, even in the visitation area with spouses or girlfriends (as covertly as possible).

And, unfortunately, drugs are available as well.

People on the outside think that just because someone is locked up that they either don't want to commit any more crime or that they can't. Sadly, many inmates, as everyone knows, when they are released go back to the same life that landed them in prison in the first place. So why would they not continue this life just because they are behind bars? Many of them are very smart and cunning and become a part of the 'social fabric' within the prison system.

Don't get me wrong, there are many inmates who are truly repentant for their crimes and try each day to survive while incarcerated. There are also many who try to go one step further and attempt to bring about some good in the world, even if their world is confined to the prison.

I have many brothers (and I call them this) who are trying every day to move past the evil that they created in their past, and to share in Christ's mercy. This is the world that I try to live and work in every day.

I'm involved in several of the many programs that are available to inmates. Lori Pompa, a professor at Temple University works with undergraduate students in a program called the *Inside Out Program*. And Villa Nova runs a program that offers scholarships to inmates. I'm involved with both at present.

Plays in the chapel and auditorium are presented here, some of which are ones that I either wrote or co-wrote with a fellow inmate. *CNN* and *60 Minutes* have been here as well to tape shows and do interviews.

I'm taking a class now called *Impact on Crime* to better understand the other side of what crime leaves behind; the victims and their loved ones and how they are effected by a crime.

[The conversation shifted several times at this point]

There's a new drug called K2 that is being smuggled in to inmates from the outside. Many of the inmates are going nuts from this. It is very dangerous.

As we already talked about, I've seen other inmates, many brothers in Christ, come and go over the years. Some, lifers like myself, have died here. Many die or are sick – too many. It saddens me to see some of my brothers fade away and die. But that is life in prison.

There is a bill, HB 2135, in the Pennsylvania House supporting parole for lifers. Now this wouldn't automatically grant parole for a lifer, but it would give an inmate an opportunity to go before a parole board and plead his case, with the possible outcome of being granted parole. I'm trying to be cautiously optimistic about this, since it is something that might take years to actually happen, and then, years more before I might be given the opportunity to come up for parole. It's a long shot, but long shots are all I have.

One of my plays, *Fight Another Day* was performed at the *Philadelphia Fight Center* by former inmates. I was humbled by the notes that I got from the audience members after the performance, praising my work and encouraging me to continue to write my plays.

Tell us about your horror movie, "Spiritual Warfare."

Spiritual Warfare was the second horror flick that I wrote. The first was *Gruesome's Legend* which is finished, but sitting on the shelf at a friend's house waiting to be released. But that's another story, which I'll get to later.

Spiritual Warfare was only half made when I came to prison. It was, in fact, made by combining two films that I was working on, *Horrorscope* and *Heavenbound*.

With the help of a friend, Larry Kirschner, a filmmaker and videographer, the rest of the film was made. He performed his magic and directed some new scenes, reused existing ones throughout the film, and added a narrator – my uncle Nick Mamallis.

The crazy thing about it is that I was both main characters, Eddie Kraven and his father Von Kraven, so Kirschner had to put together new scenes from existing footage. Another interesting thing about it is that it is made up of various types of film: 8 mm, 16 mm, digital, and others.

[Despite some choppiness due to these things it still did pretty well this past October at an independent filmmakers' film festival in Los Angeles. It's now available on Vimeo.]

Another friend has the film *Gruesome's Legend* right now. He owns 49% of it and I own the rest. We worked together on it and are now in the process of blowing the dust off and putting it out in the world for people to see. Hopefully, that will happen sometime soon.

I'm amazed at how much you have accomplished and continue to do while in prison. I would suspect many of your fellow inmates are not as productive as you have been.

It isn't as different in that respect from the outside as you might believe. Sure, there are those who have other things on their minds besides being productive, but there are also those who are trying to make a positive impact, even though they may spend the rest of their life in prison.

Tell us about your family, your mom and dad, your sister. What was it like growing up for you and your sister?

My mom had an abusive past. From what I've heard, when her mother and father divorced and he remarried, the woman he married was abusive to my mother. She even locked her out of the house after her father died.

By the time her father died, uncle Nick was out of the house and starting his own family. My mom was a teenager then.

After my mom and dad married and Michelle and I were still very young, they had two more children, Shawn and Diane. Both died when they were still infants. Shawn's death took its toll on the marriage, but when Diane came along new hope arose. But then she died as well.

This tore my parents apart. My mom started having an affair with a guy named Jon. He was a man she worked with when she worked in the diner at the Philly airport.

He was cruel to her and Michelle and me as well. He once threw her on railroad tracks while they were on their way to work together. He used to whip Michelle and me with a bullwhip when we did anything wrong.

She returned to my dad for a short period of time. My mom then left my dad again and she took the two of us kids to Nashville, Tennessee to follow her dream of becoming a country western singer. We stayed with a woman named Christy, who had two teenage daughters 15 and 16 years old. She was the mistress of a famous country singer, according to my mom.

Every night we were given potato soup to eat; Michelle usually threw it up.

Our mom was working as a barmaid and was a backup singer for Hank Williams Jr. I was six and Michelle was five.

Michelle was beaten physically by Christy's two daughters and I was abused sexually. One daughter abused us and the other watched.

When we went back to Philly our mom bartended and an 18-year-old girl who lived with her mom in the same apartment complex babysat Michelle and me. She made us run around the apartment naked; she would also be naked. She made me perform sexual acts on her and even tried to make me have sex with her; but I wasn't capable of that at my age.

She threatened us that if we told then a cross would burn onto our chests. But Michelle eventually told our mom and she confronted the babysitter and her mom.

No police report or charges were filed. Our mom didn't want to report it. I guess she was so humiliated to have that happen to her children without her knowing about it or doing anything for so long a time.

Mom and dad got back together shortly after this. Dad cooked at the Four-Star Restaurant in Concordville, PA for a couple of years.

Also during this time Michelle was hit by a car, but she survived.

My parents, for all their faults, were a kind and generous couple. Despite having little of their own they used to help other people. They would bring people into our home and feed them and give them a place to stay for a while.

My mom did pursue her singing career for a while. She made a couple of recordings and some were played on the radio. She told me later that she made an album.

Mom ran a restaurant that was also called the Four-Star Restaurant, but in a different town than my dad's. So, they lived apart. I lived with my dad and Michelle lived with mom.

*   *   *

14

The Interview – Part 2

Larry, you kind of jumped from pre-teen to high school age. What about the years in between? What can you tell us about that time period?

In 1981, when I was 15, I sang in the school choir. I started seeing a girl named Carrie, who had a crush on me. George was her dad and he once told me, "If you f**k my daughter, I'll kill you!"

During 1981 and '82 I dated her for five months. Her dad took me to Lancaster to a hotel to rape me on several occasions. He also forced himself on me in his car one time when he was driving me home from seeing Carrie.

That was when I said, "No more!" I would not let anyone abuse me ever again.

That experience, and the chaos I saw at home, unfortunately are the only memories I have of that time in my life. Sad, isn't it?

My mom was domineering; she would break up any relationship I had with girls. She would call the girl and harass her over and over until she broke up with me. This went on from my high school years through my adult years working in theater and on movies to even when Stefan and I got together.

[Stromberg pauses and reflects further on his life; back to an earlier time.]

There were dogs and cats, boxes and piles of garbage and other things all around my house growing up; I was embarrassed to bring any of my friends over.

Mom and dad separated again; mom was working in Fonsville and dad was working at the *Corn Crib*.

At that time, a guy named Frank (not real name) dated my sister Michelle. She was on heavy drugs and alcohol at the age of 16. She was living in Devon.

One time my mom and Michelle were supposed to pick up dad at the train station after work. But Michelle and mom had an argument as mom was leaving work, getting into her car. Michelle hit her in the head with a brick. Michelle was messed up on drugs.

Another time Michelle and a friend of hers tried to poison my mom; but they failed.

When I was 17 or 18 I moved to Upper Darby, Pennsylvania and worked at a Kmart. I was raised a Catholic, but became a Christian (non-denominational) and worked out and played sports. That was my life; that and going to acting school. I attended the *John Barth Acting School* on Chestnut Street in Philly.

[Having been an English major I had to ask.]

Do you mean John Barth the novelist and short story writer of "Lost in the Funhouse" fame; the professor at the University of Buffalo, my old hometown?

No, John Barth, the actor, of "Crazy Glue" and "Tidy Bowl" fame!

[We all had a good laugh at this.]

I also went to *Peter Schuyler Acting School* in New York City for 11 weeks where I had one-on-one classes.

In Lansdowne, Pennsylvania I met Jerry Rath, who was the owner of the *Lansdowne Movie Theater*. I was looking for a place to rehearse my play called *The Wrong Bank* and film it. He told me that if I cleaned out the attic and basement he would let me use his theater to rehearse and film in.

The Wrong Bank was a short comedy that I wrote about a would-be bank robber who breaks into this bank only to find that he was about to rob a blood bank. My friend Larry Kirschner shot this for me. There was even an article in the paper about it.

It was after this that I wrote *Gruesome's Legend*. This is a horror film that I did with a friend. It sits on a shelf now; we completed it in 1987. I'm hoping to get that released in the near future. We just need to work out a few details.

I was in a horror-comedy film when I was 21. It's called *Blades* and is a tale of a runaway lawnmower that runs people over. I was one of its victims.

I got involved in Community Theater. There I met a woman, a make-up artist named Lyn (not her real name). I started to date her, but my mom would fight with me about dating her. She would call her a tramp; she told me that Lyn wasn't good enough for me; the same as she had with all the other girlfriends that I had or even girls that I tried to date.

It got so bad that my mom would call Lyn up and threaten her. This is what she would do to other women I wanted to date; and later she did this to Stefan.

While I worked in theater and any jobs I could get in film or TV, I worked at the *Riverside Fitness Center*, the place where I met Stefan. It was in 1989 that I began work there.

In the early 1990s I had a small part in the movie, *Rocky V*. I also appeared in, *I Don't Buy Kisses Anymore*, with Jason Alexander (from the *Seinfeld* show), *Money for Nothing*, with Joh Cusack, and *The Distinguished Gentleman*, with Eddie Murphy.

Granted, they were small parts, but that's what actors that want to land big rolls do – they show what they can do, and maybe get a break.

While I had pretty steady work in film and TV, and worked at the fitness center as a trainer, I also worked on my own films – horror films; namely, *Gruesome's Legend* and the two (*Horrorscope* and *Heavenbound*) that became one, *Spiritual Warfare* and wrote plays and screenplays.

All the while that I worked on all these things, I still read the Bible and prayed every day.

While I was looking for the right girl to marry, and the search being hampered by my mother, my sister, Michelle, had been married three times. Our lives, while still close, had very different directions at that time. It seemed that the abuse and hard life that she had experienced so far had led her to drugs, alcohol, several marriages, and incarceration. But the one thing that she gained was a beautiful daughter who is fulfilling the promise that Michelle and I once saw for ourselves.

I, on the other hand, stayed focused on my acting, writing, training and finding Jesus Christ in my life.

Sometimes our faith gets tested and we fail – as I did. But as God forgives and gives us renewed life in his son, we have the chance to atone for our sins, no matter how great. I've been given that chance now that I have found the Lord. My demons could only control me when my faith was not strong. I built up my body, but not my soul; and that had been more abused than my body. And I didn't ever realize that until it was too late for dear Stefan and Paula.

[He paused a moment; a sad expression fell over him. Then he began again.]

But Michelle and I did have good times together. She worked with me on my films and as children we played together, because sometimes each other was all we had.

It was in 1993 that I met Stefan. Then, she lived in the apartment on West Walnut Lane in Germantown that I would later move into and call home – at least for three years.

153

We had some good neighbors that we called friends. Even the Super, whose name is also Larry, was a good guy. In fact, he still runs the old mansion (as of 2016).

The street was lined with old mansions that had been converted into separate apartments. Ours had a swimming pool in the back, where I loved to swim.

Once, before I moved in with her, while Stefan and I were in the shower, I told her how I had been sexually abused as a child. It was after that that I told my mom and dad.

Stefan and I were spending a great deal of time together now and it was in that shower that I, for the first time, experienced the culmination of what love-making is.

While Stefan and I were finding love, and growing together as one, my mom was there trying to break us apart. She called Stefan 40 or 50 times threatening her, calling her all kinds of names.

It was then that I moved in with Stefan. My mom was devastated, angry with me that I could do that to her. My mother was determined to break us apart no matter what. This went on for the short six weeks that Stefan and I knew each other.

Louisville was where Stefan grew up and went to school, until she went to Temple University in Philly.

We visited her dad and decided right then that we would get married. We put together a very impromptu wedding and went back to Philadelphia husband and wife.

Those were the happiest six weeks of my life. There were more to come, but it seems that there was a downward slide that I wasn't aware of happening shortly after we went back to Philly and things settled into a normal routine; at least what might be seen as a normal routine.

With my busy schedule and hers as well, it was hard to find a 'normal' routine; but I guess it's that way for many young couples just starting out.

I had my acting career and she had her jewelry-making business; both in addition to our steady jobs – mine as a trainer at the fitness center, and hers as a social worker at Temple Hospital.

I now see that I spent too much time on myself, now that I can look back at my mistakes. I worked at the fitness center, worked on my horror films (writing, directing and acting in), took any and all acting jobs that I could find, on stage and in film; even in commercials. In what free time I had, I spent some of that surrounded by friends. I wasn't ready for marriage; I thought that my life could go on just as it had.

There was a price to pay for not paying the attention to my new bride that I should have. Her old boyfriend, Bob, would visit her, sometimes in the middle of the night. This annoyed me to no end.

[Our conversation took a sudden turn. We could see that the current topic was getting too emotional for him. So, we talked more about his family history.]

Tell us about your roots; your family history. Has your family always lived in the Philadelphia area?

My father's side of the family lived in Baltimore. My grandparents were named Bernie and Helen Stromberg. After they were married they moved to Upper Darby, Delaware County, PA.

They had six children, five boys and one girl.

My dad and mom married in 1965 and had four children; me, Michelle, Shawn and Diane. Both Shawn and Diane died as infants.

On my mother's side of the family it's a little more complicated. My grandparents' names were Nick and Clara Mamallis. It had been an arranged marriage and he was older than her. They married and lived in Baltimore as well, where they had my uncle Nick and my mother, Diane.

At one point my grandmother wanted a divorce. My grandfather got the two children, remarried and moved to Philadelphia where he became Captain of Police in the town of Millbourne, in Delaware County, PA. He drowned in a boating accident on a nearby lake in 1964. The circumstances surrounding his death were never clear. There may have been some foul play; no one seems to know – or wants to tell.

Clara, my maternal grandmother remarried and had a daughter, Ramona. This second husband, Jack, died and she married for a third time. Her third husband died three years after her in 2005.

[The conversation transitioned to his passion – acting.]

Tell us about some of the films and theater productions you've been in.

[A big smile came across his lips as he seemed to slip back into happier times].

I was in a sci-fi movie called *Master Race from Mars*. I played a drunken sailor. It was a fun movie.

156

I worked in *12 Monkeys* with Bruce Willis, *Bogus* with Haley Joel Osment and Whoopie Goldberg, *Up Close and Personal* with Robert Redford and Michele Pfeiffer, and *IQ* with Walter Matheau and Meg Ryan to name a few of the big money movies.

On stage I played Tony in *Tony and Tina's Wedding* and was in *I Love My Wife*.

[No matter how we tried to move the conversation away from it, Stromberg was drawn back to his life with Stefan. He wanted to tell us all; he needed to relive that part of his life – the moments, good and bad.]

In December 1995 Stefan went to Florida to visit her mom. She didn't want me to go with her. She drove her truck, alone.

While she was gone, I guess I didn't notice, but I lost weight. I began some obsessive-compulsive behaviors. I called her four times a day. I went to my therapist, Bryan Cohen; I called his mother, Dr. Sandy Cohen (Stefan's therapist).

It's odd, but as busy as I was when she was with me, I felt a huge void when she was away.

I sent her jewelry and I filled the house with flowers and balloons when she came home. She was gone only three weeks, but it seemed like a lifetime to me.

I bought tickets for us to see *Hello Saigon* in New York City for her birthday, but she chose to stay in Florida instead.

When she returned home she went back to work at *Long's Gourmet Chinese Restaurant* downtown. It was when she had returned and got back into her routine that she told me. She told me that she was pregnant. She said that the baby was fathered by the Asian cook that she worked with at the restaurant.

I remember that moment as if it just happened. And it plays, over and over, just as every one of those sick, horrible moments never go away. Mostly, they fill me with regret for the actions that I took when they happened.

I remember when she told me of the pregnancy she said, "You can kill me now."

But she still wanted me to stay. There was an obsession with each other that we both felt. We kept being drawn together. It was as if we were out to destroy ourselves and each other at the same time.

I began hearing voices and seeing things – voices of anger – "You should kill her!" "You should kill yourself!"

I began to see shadows in the apartment. I felt a demonic presence. It was all connected to my abused past and acting in horror movies.

Stefan complained to me that she felt that I was praying too much. She didn't know that I was praying for my life. My prayer was for my sanity and to release me from the demons that had my soul captured.

Stefan was Jewish, but not a believer; not a practicing Jew. So, religion was not a real conflict in our relationship, other than my praying too much towards the end.

When Stefan went to Ft. Lauderdale she drove down and was there for three weeks and then flew back to Philadelphia.

After she told me about the baby, she flew back to Florida for an abortion without asking if I would want her to have it and raise it as our own. In fact, she later told me that she thought it was mine; maybe to make me more crazy. I don't know. A neighbor of ours named Janice (not her real name) later said to me that the newspaper reported that the baby was mine.

She went to Florida a second time and stayed with her mother when she had the abortion. Stefan called from Florida New Year's Day and said, "I love you, Larry. We'll try to work everything out."

It was the beginning of a new year, 1996, and what I hoped would be a new beginning for the two of us. Instead it was the beginning of the end; an end that would come in four short, tumultuous months.

*   *   *

15

Life Behind the Razor Wire

During our visit Stromberg discussed what life was like in prison; what he has witnessed – the good, the bad and the tragic. We talked about his 20 years of incarceration: 19 years at S.C.I. Coal Township and now beginning his second year at S.C.I. Graterford.

In previous phone conversations, he gave some general notion of what it was like, but seemed not to be too comfortable in discussing this subject from a prison phone. So, instead, he wrote about it, and, while at S.C.I. Graterford in a face-to-face interview with him, he felt freer to openly discuss the topic.

From his letter, and the interview with Stromberg, here are some of the things he related about "Life behind the Razor Wire" (borrowed from the title of one of his plays). In his own words:

*   *   *

I have seen stabbings from gang members seeking revenge for one reason or another; it might have been an insult, a threat or even a territorial thing.

I have seen rapes; they occur in many different places in the prison. Most people that watch movies showing scenes in prison see rapes occurring mostly in the shower, but when we shower we wear sweat shorts – we're never fully naked there.

I've seen food strikes in the whole prison; you can't imagine how this can disrupt the system.

I have seen people die as I worked as a medical janitor at Coal Township. Some die of natural causes, others not so natural.

When you're a lifer, there's only one way out and that's feet first. That's a cold expression, but a true one. The cold, hard reality for a lifer is that's how it happens. You may live a long time, but eventually get old and sick and die.

I have had many over the past 20 years that I have called brother who have gone on to God's glory.

While in prison I have had friends, those who have worked with me on plays and those who I see and talk to daily, commit suicide. Without a reason to live many choose to die. They might see it as a never-ending spinning on a wheel, like a rat or a mouse in a cage. The wheel keeps turning, but goes nowhere. But they fail to see that they can make a difference in life, even in here. That God's gift is what we can bring to others in this world. They have lost hope and faith. It's very sad to witness. I try each day to give a positive outlook to others around me.

I've been blessed by having people in both prisons who have believed in me and have given me support and encouragement. People like Rev. Comick and Rev. Torres to name two of the many who help to motivate me in my playwriting and performances. I try to bring that same sense of hope and encouragement to those around me who are in need of it.

I've seen guards set inmates up because of the color of their skin or because of their crime.

I've seen men have sex with other men as I worked as a block worker in the county prison.

I've seen men go crazy over a transgender inmate coming on the prison block.

I've seen guards having sex with inmates when I accidentally walk in on them as a janitor in the medical department and in the educational building. Most people on the outside think that the guards are all men; they're not.

I've had a few staff members approaching me sexually; both female and male. I always declined any staff member in any sexual act. I just wanted to stay close to God and do my plays for his glory. Don't get me wrong, some of the female staff that I got to know over the years were truly beautiful. But, I didn't have any sexual relations.

A lot of people think that men in prison, especially for violent crimes, are tough, close-lipped, no nonsense kinds of guys. But, what might be a shock to many, gossip is a big thing in prison.

Everyone knows everything about everybody. Especially their crimes. Everyone knows everything about the staff, the guards, teachers and other staff members as well.

Working in medical I have seen men die, rot away from cancer and nobody to collect their remains when they die. So, I was told their remains were cremated and thrown in the trash.

That seems a real sin against humanity; how worthless we must seem to some people.

While all of us here, who are serving time have our sins, and deserve punishment, you would think that in death we are all equal and deserving of some decency, if only for our remains.

Once I saw a man die in the back dorm at Coal Township and the other men in the dorm stole what they could from the dead man's body.

I have seen many men go home only to return to prison very quickly. Recidivism is a fact of life in prison. From the outside, you see a man (or woman) come out of prison, try to assimilate back into the population, but fail. They commit another crime, because that's all they know how to do to survive and then are sent back to prison. On the inside, we see a brother (or sister) get set free with the hopes that they can cope with this new-found freedom; that they have a safe and supportive setting to return to so that they don't fall back into the trap of a criminal life that got them here in the first place.

But far too many have little or no support on the outside, except for the people that helped them get here before. If they have no positive support, then they rely on the criminal element that they knew before. It starts a cycle that only ends with them serving longer sentences that sometimes ends with them dying in prison; either by assaults from other prisoners, illness, suicide or other ways.

Ironically, I have also known many men who have died when they went back home. Some of illnesses, others from being around the wrong people, and still others taking their own lives.

In the medical department at Coal Township, where I was a janitor, I saw many inmates drink their own urine and eat and smear their feces over their bodies due to mental illness.

I have seen the horrible hurt when someone losses a loved one in prison. I know the pain myself, losing my dad, grandmothers, cousins and friends. Even the deaths of my dogs and cats hurt me deeply. For I wish I never did the crime that hurt as many lives.

I've seen many with deep remorse for their crimes. They suffer from their own deeds as do those that they harmed and their families. Many of the men I see every day wish only one thing – that they could undo the harm they did to others.

And I have seen many others that have no remorse; they have no desire to change themselves or how they feel about their crime(s).

As a routine part of life in prison you are strip searched when you have a visit and there are also cell searches from time to time. I hate these; we have so little personal privacy or space as it is. But much like outside the walls in your world, there are those who make certain things required because of their actions. That's why so many laws are made, because of the few that are always trying to beat the system. It is no different inside. There are written rules and unwritten rules here as well.

A life sentence is called "The Wheel," because round and round we go. And I have met men who have been in prison for 40 and 50 years with no relief in sight, except death. And I know many who are just waiting to die.

Some of the sadder things that I see are the mentally ill who need help. They just walk around the prison like zombies, not getting proper treatment; zoned out on heavy medication – walking dead men.

By the grace of God, I've been able to stage over 60 plays for the glory of God. I'm forever grateful. Looking back these 20 years, I remember the D.A. said I would never act or direct again. But God said YES! (only by his grace and love).

I've never had a write-up in prison, I've done programs, gained education, stayed in shape and became a better human being, full of remorse. I've made great friends along the way, as well.

While it is truly hard time, God has provided me with a path that allows me to help others inside and outside the prison in so many different ways. I have good family members and friends who help by support, love and encouragement, as well as, promoting my mission to help others who might go wrong in their lives.

I have many brothers here in prison who act in my plays during church services and other events we have. There are staff members who support and promote my work and that of others who look for creative outlets.

Like any other person, I have some things that I call favorites. My favorite book is the Bible, which I read every day. Being an actor I have a whole range of favorite movies and actors from *On the Waterfront* to *The Godfather* (both Marlon Brando pics), and *Jaws* to *Platoon*. I get to watch some of my favorite sports teams (all from Philly): The Eagles, Flyers, Sixers and the Phillies.

I miss the ocean and live theater, but most of all I miss my dad's pizza; it was the best.

*   *   *

Prayers for Forgiveness

A great many prisoners are remorseful; some because they got caught, while others because they have seen the evil of their past life and truly wish to change for the better.

My remorse comes from ending the lives of two people I really loved; from not being able to stop myself from committing this horrific deed.

I didn't really plan this, but was driven to this by a lifetime of abuse from every direction.

Here are some words about this:

[To Stefan and Paula]

Dear Stefan and Paula,

I have re-lived that night over and over again when I took your lives in such a horrible way. I still hear your screams in my head.

One thing I know for a fact is that you're both in Heaven; you're with the Lord. A place of beauty and true peace.

You know that I had a full-blown psychotic break. This is no excuse; it's the truth.

I am forever remorseful for what I did to you both and your family. Words can't express my deep sorrow. My shame. My guilt.

I can only imagine what you're lives would have been if this never happened. If I would have just let you go and walked away for us both. For your family. For my family.

I've tried to do good with my life to help others. I guess this is my purpose now: Humanity.

Humanity; God has called me to do this. I have faced all the full consequences for my actions against you, your family and society. I am forever sorry. Forever. I hope you can forgive me. For I can't forgive myself. I'm sorry.

Soul to soul,
Love and peace,
Larry

*　　　*　　　*

16

Spiritual Warfare

One Man's Journey

In one of our many written correspondences I asked Stromberg to talk about any issue we so far neglected to touch on. Because, like most people, I haven't had the kind of experiences in life that would afford me the insight and full understanding of a person who commits such a crime. Thank God.

By having an open discussion about any and everything my hopes were to better understand where he came from (emotionally and psychologically) and where these 20 years have led him to today.

*　　*　　*

I'm a man full of regret and remorse.
Why would I allow myself to have a psychotic break?
How could I commit such a horrific crime?

Why would I destroy my life, my dreams and come to prison for a life sentence?

How could I hurt so many people, including Stefan and Paula's family?

How could I hurt my family and not be there for the people I love? My mother, sister, niece, grandparents; and not be there for my father when he had his heart attack?

Why would I feel the pain of losing loves in prison?

Why would I want to lose friends and destroy my acting and film career?

Why would I leave my beautiful dogs (Spartagus and Bandit) and my new apartment?

Why did I stay with a woman who would have multiple affairs?

Why couldn't I just stay away from Stefan and move on with my new life I could have had without her?

I know now mental issues is a major factor without question. Sexual addiction is another one. Betrayal and extreme hurt, pain, anxiety, obsession, anger, spiritual attacks from demons and hearing voices over and over again in my head to kill.

I prayed and prayed, but, in the end, I gave in to the dark side. When I think back now, all I had to do is move out and leave; that's how easy it was.

Why did I need to have Stefan back even with her sexual unfaithfulness?

I know it's all from mental illness, sexual abuse, spiritual attacks from demons and being betrayed.

It all came upon me like a whirlwind.

There were some parallels between my life at that time and the script I had written and was in the process of filming, *Spiritual Warfare*.

The film, I believe, is about me in my subconscious and in the spiritual world. It's the battle of good vs. evil; God and the Devil; light and darkness; sanity and insanity; seeing Angels and being in battle with Demons.

We are dealing with schizophrenia and extreme paranoid personality disorder with anxiety and bi-polar disorders, both Eddie Kraven (*in the movie*) and me (*in real life*).

Being like Eddie Kraven, a man with a horrible childhood and past, and a man who makes horrible mistakes in his life. That was both of us. I guess I wrote his story, but it was just as much mine.

Much like this character, I was dealing with the supernatural and seeking forgiveness, purpose and peace in Christ alone; but neither he nor I knew how to find it.

Both Eddie and I were trying to overcome sexual, mental and physical abuse. We were looking for peace in a horribly abusive childhood.

Unlike Eddie, whose father Von Kraven was cruel and abusive – pure evil, my childhood wasn't always bad, only the abuse was bad.

My mother and father always loved me and Michelle. We were blessed and they loved us very much.

170

I believe the abuse caused a form of mental illness in my life. Acting and working out covered up the pain. Stefan was someone I thought and believed I would be happy with. When I really found out about her betrayal, I became like Eddie Kraven. Then I became more like Von Kraven, the evil father of Eddie. Finally, I fell back into the character of Eddie, seeking redemption.

Today, serving a life sentence with no chance for parole, I'm grateful to have accomplished some good things to better myself as a human being.

As I stated earlier, I try to better myself by becoming involved in programs, such as *Violence Prevention and Impact on Crime, Restorative Justice* that teaches the impact of crime to the victims, the offender's family, the victim's family and the community. I am taking college courses to help me further my writing skills and knowledge of things that I never dreamed of before.

I better myself by writing, acting and directing plays behind bars for a greater cause – to help change lives for the glory of God. I'm grateful for my film being out for others to see.

I hope to better myself for my family to see a good man who only made a bad choice – a horrible choice. To be a better son, brother, uncle, nephew and friend to all.

Better myself by my faith in Christ and being honest with all my faults in life.

Better myself for Stefan and Paula to see a changed life from the other side of Heaven.

Better myself for working hard for 42 cents/hour at my jobs assigned to me in prison by the employment office.

All I see is sadness from the past, hoping by the grace of God for a second chance and see the ocean again.

All I can say is how remorseful I am to Stefan and Paula's family; to their friends; to my family and friends.

I am heartbroken and I'll try to help others to not make the same mistakes through my plays for Christ and with my life.

I'm learning to forgive and I pray to be forgiven. I'm seeking redemption; I'm seeking to be forgiven.

I'm seeking God's presence in my life, everyday till I reach heaven. Heaven is a perfect place of love!

*   *   *

In many of our conversations I can hear the enthusiasm he has for the work that he is doing, and how others around him (other inmates and staff members alike) have come to accept their roles in life and are finding the good and positive things that they can embrace.

I also hear the regret he has, in every conversation, every letter and email, and in every play that he writes for the glory of God for having murdered two people whom he loved and who were loved by many others. Two people who had no reason to die, and every reason to live.

Nothing can bring them back and he faces that every day, in every waking moment. But rather than fall into constant depression, he has found a purpose.

Everyone has things in their lives that they regret; some more serious than others; but we all do. The people we've hurt or wronged; the lies or deceptions we've lived; the temptations that we've succumbed to. We all have them in our past, or possibly even our present.

His is one that haunts him daily, and yet inspires him to make amends for by giving to others; by helping those who are falling as far as he once did.

In one of his dreams, just before the murders, he saw himself falling into a black abyss when a hand reached out to save him. He recognized it as the hand of Jesus Christ. Only he let go too soon after this vision.

Christ gives us a hand of help when we need it most, but it is up to us to hang on and not let go. That is our free will.

Larry Stromberg was in such a deep state of despair that he couldn't hold on long enough to be saved. But Jesus never gives up. His hand is always there for us to reach out and take hold of if we are willing to.

Stromberg has now done that, and he is holding on tightly, hoping never to let go again.

The story doesn't end here; this is only the beginning of what was a very rough and rocky road. Now the path is clear and the light is bright. What will come is unknown for any of us. But what will continue is the way of God. A life inside or outside of these prison walls working to help others find their true way in life; a journey that started out badly and declined into madness and despair, now follows the light of Christ that guides the way home.

Stromberg's story is not unique in and of itself; it is a story of (sadly) too many men and women in life today. Not all end the same way, and not all end.

His life has had several distinct phases that have led to the next. As with all things that happen to any of us in life, our future actions are guided by their success or failure. In his, the abuse succeeded in bringing about several emotional and mental issues that led him to commit the crime he did. The treatment that he so badly needed and never received allowed for all the evil to take over his life. It's very sad how the help he now receives could have possibly averted the deaths of two people he loved.

But out of the ashes of despair arose a *Phoenix*; the ashes of a man whose life had false direction and even faultier guidance. Now, even behind the walls and bars of man, he has come to know Christ and a loving relationship with his creator, God Almighty.

Maybe all our experiences bring us to our true purpose in life; or maybe our purpose is defined by the needs that bring us to those experiences; or possibly God has a plan for each of us, and it is our responsibility to find it and fulfill that promise.

Whatever the answer is, Larry Stromberg has for a purpose and a destiny that God has given to him – to help others find their way to the Lord and avoid the evils that are trying to overtake them.

Stromberg now knows that if his skills as an actor and writer can bring someone closer to God and help them avoid those acts that will lead them to where he now is, then his life will have meaning – in or out of prison.

While each day brings him closer to **Death by Incarceration**, the hope of one day being out in the world again, brings him one step closer to fulfilling his mission in life and spread his ministry with his plays of redemption through his **Redemption Theater Ministry.**

Stromberg now has a lawyer looking at possible remedies for him. Additionally, the Pennsylvania State Legislature has a bill that has been proposed to allow for possibility of parole for lifers. Pennsylvania House Bill 2135, introduced by State Rep. Dawkins, would allow for Stromberg to one day be eligible for parole.

He also has the right to petition for a pardon or commutation of his sentence from the Governor of Pennsylvania. So, he still holds the hope that one day he will be a free man; free to take his ministry and his plays of redemption out into a world that sorely needs redeeming.

*   *   *

Following is a short play that he recently wrote and performed before an audience at The State Correctional Institution at Graterford, Pennsylvania.

The play is called "The Dual" and can be found on the Prisons Foundation website.

The Dual

Only a chair is on the empty stage at center stage.
An angelic voice is heard in the background.

Angelic Voice: (V.O.)
"Put on the whole armour of God, that ye may be able to stand against the wiles of the devil.

For we wrestle not against flesh and blood, but against principalities, against powers, against the rulers of the darkness of this world, against spiritual wickedness in high places.

Wherefore take unto you the whole armour of God, that ye may be able to withstand in the evil day, and having done all to stand."

Ephesians 6: 11-13

The angelic voice ends.
A lone man walks unto the stage from stage left and takes a seat on the chair at center stage. He takes a deep breath and looks forward with intense eyes as he begins to speak.

Lone Man:

So far, it's been a good day. (*Pause*) There's been a sense of real peace, harmony and tranquility all around me and in my mind. I feel safe and secure from the warfare all around me in the unseen world. The spiritual realm. The battle that's in the true supernatural and the spiritual warfare that we're all in as believers in the Lord Jesus Christ. (*Pause*) I must be prayed up and in the word of God every day. Every day I live on this earth. "Take unto you, the helmet of salvation, the sword of the spirit; which is the word of God."

The man stands up.

Lone Man:

This is what is needed to fight off all the attacks and the assaults from the evil one and his army of demons. The devil thrives on tormenting me with my past and with unforgiving thoughts towards myself and others who have hurt and betrayed me. With the lust of my eyes. The lust of the flesh and the pride of life.

The man paces back and forth.

Lone Man:
That's why I have the word of God imbedded in my heart at all times to battle Satan when he comes to condemn and tempt me. When that evil voice whispers in my ear to judge me. Condemning me with my past sins that hurt so many.

The Lone Man stops at Center Stage.

Lone Man:
With lustful temptation and evil thoughts that seem to come out of nowhere. Some say this is a voice only in my mind.

The Lone Man looks forward with intense, hurtful eyes.

Lone Man:
A form of mental illness or just my subconscious speaking to me based on my inability to forgive myself and others who have hurt me in the past. But, I know it's only the voice of the devil himself. An all-out war. (*Pause*) That's why I'm grateful for the loving, comforting voice of the Holy Spirit filled with love and true encouragement. The voice of the comforter.

The man sits back down.

Lone Man:
So, there's a dual going on. A war for my soul. The dual between good and evil from within. A fight between light and darkness. Between God and the devil. I know light will always win.

177

Goodness will triumph. God is all powerful. (*Pause*) Still, the devil wants to destroy my testimony in Christ and the evil one wants to kill me. Kill us all. Satan doesn't want me to help others to know and accept the loving grace of Jesus Christ. To hear that still small voice of the Holy Spirit informing me that I am loved and that I am forgiven. That I am a child of the all-powerful, all-loving and all-knowing, awesome God of the universe. So, I stay still and get to know God on a personal in-depth level. (*Pause*) Satan never gives up. He's relentless and hates the chosen ones of Christ. He's full of contempt and despises me. The devil takes pure pleasure in the dual. Satan enjoys the game. He gets off on it. It becomes exhilarating to him.

That's when the man stands up slowly to the left side and then he cracks his neck. Twists his fingers. Takes deep breaths and then begins to growl. Then he speaks with a very sinister tone in his voice. He speaks to the invisible Lone Man in the chair.

Evil Voice:
It's me. Hmmmmmmm! It's so wonderful that you do acknowledge me. This makes me so damn happy. So much joy, huh? (*Pause*) I know you, my friend. I know all about your sin. Your lust. What you desire most. I know about your shame and about your immense regret. Your anger and rage. I love you, my dear friend. (*Laughs*) Ha, ha, ha, ha, ha. Don't you love me? Hmmm? I do enjoy tempting you with what you desire most. I do. Yes. (*Laughs*) Ha, ha, ha, ha. Yes, indeed. You belong to me. Don't you ever forget that. You did my dreadful bidding in your life. Thank you for all the evil rotten things you've done to hurt and destroy so many. You rotten to the core sinner. You can never get rid of

me, you damn fool. Never! You destroyed everything you ever loved, you stupid idiot! You are mine. All mine. Now and forever. (*Pause*) I am god. For I will never leave you nor forsake you. You belong to me.

The man sits back down in the chair, covering his ears.

Lone Man:
No more. Please, no more...

The man breaks down in tears.

Lone Man:
Help me, Lord Jesus! I'm not a victim of the devils' scheme no more! I choose to fight with faith! I'm heavy laden. Give me rest and peace. Comfort me, Holy Spirit.

He uncovers his ears and sits up straight.

Lone Man:
My redeemer! My savior! I call upon thee, Lord God almighty! I want your loving presence!

The man slowly stands up to the right side of the chair. A very peaceful demeanor is seen in the man.

Holy Spirit:
Greater is he that is in you, than he in the world. I'm here, my son. I'm always here. Just call upon me and I will answer you and show great and mighty things which thou knowest not. You

are safe in my loving arms. My loving arms of peace, joy, hope, grace and true love that's unfailing.

The Holy Spirit speaks with a Godly tone in his voice.

Holy Spirit:
You are loved. You are forgiven. Redeemed. You are saved and your salvation is secured for everlasting. You are more than a conqueror in Christ Jesus. And nothing, I mean nothing, will be able to separate you from my love. Nothing. The love of God. (*Pause*) So, fight the good fight of faith. For the just shall live by faith. Rebuke the devil in the name of Jesus Christ and he must flee every time. Say, the Lord rebukes you. But, you know this, for the word of God directs you to this truth, my child. I will lead you into all truth and understanding. (*Pause*) You are loved, my son. You belong to me. For, I will never leave you, nor forsake you.

The Holy Spirit becomes silent. The man sits down full of joy.

Lone Man:
Thank you, Lord. Thank you for your love.

He sits thanking God. Then he stands back up fast to the left side with a fury. In madness.

Evil Voice:
Oh, please. Stop with the nonsense, will you, huh? God doesn't love you. He hates you! Look what he did to me!!!! He's lying to you. You are the scum of the earth. You are a piece of

human trash. You belong to me. Don't get it twisted. I am the god of this world. You are mine. All mine.

He sits back down…
The man speaks with Godly boldness.

Lone Man:

You are the father of all lies, Satan! I am a child of the most high. For there is no condemnation to them which are in Christ Jesus! The Lord rebukes you in the name of Jesus Christ! The King of Kings! The Lord of Lords! Emanuel! God with us! Be gone, devil in the name of Jesus! My Lord and savior!

The man sits there in silence. harmony, peace. He takes a deep breath and speaks.

Lone Man:

Yes, the dual is on-going. But, we have the victory in Christ. For God has not given us a spirit of fear, but of power, love and of a sound mind.

The man stands up full of faith.

Lone Man:

We can win the dual with Christ. (*Pause*) For Jesus Christ is Lord.

The man exits stage left.

*   *   *

In more recent months Stromberg has been asked to participate in a recording of music and other performance arts. This recording was made at S.C.I. Graterford in May 2017. Its title is, "Songs in the Key of Free", and is available for viewing on Facebook.

On this recording Stromberg wrote and performed one of his short, one-man plays entitled, "I'm Free Within". Here, I have presented it in poetic form.

I'm Free Within

When I stage plays, and get lost in music, I'm Free.
I'm Free from my past;
Free from my mistakes;
I'm Free from my regrets; free from my shame.
Free from the loss – and pain;
I'm Free Within.

Free to be me. Free in my creativity.
Free to encourage others; Free to go on.
Free to live; Free to forgive.
I'm Free to forgive myself.
Free to cry; Free to smile again.
Free to love myself.

I'm Free to fly and soar; Free to dream.
If I'm blessed to do what I love, then I'm Free.
I'm Free Within.
Truly Free inside;
I'm Free.
I'm Free.

Where life leads Stromberg at this point is anybody's guess. But with a positive attitude and a strong faith in the Lord, I'm sure his message of faith, hope and personal responsibility will resonate within and without the walls of man.

Whether or not he is ever able to live outside of prison, his words will. Through his movies and performances, both performed by others and taped performances he is able to do, his message of redemption and love will reach a vast audience.

For those whose lives he has impacted by the two murdered women, he may never be forgiven; and that's understandable. But for those whose lives he touches and possibly saves, his life now has a whole different meaning.

Time will tell how Stromberg's work these past 20 years will be remembered set against his horrific crime.

The words of a truly great writer, William Shakespeare, from his play, *Julius Caesar*, echo in the shadow of Stromberg's great tragedy, where we hear Mark Antony state a sad fact about how people are often remembered. Antony bemoans, "The evil men do lives after them; the good is oft interred with their bones…"

Will Stromberg be remembered only for that one night of madness, or will his life since then have any meaning or redemptive qualities? Only time will tell. Regardless, he moves forward each day trying to bring hope and salvation to those (much like he was) in need of a hand stretched out to help pull them out of their own black abyss.

Works Cited

Chapter 1:

    1. In the Supreme Court of Pennsylvania, Philadelphia District. Commonwealth of Pennsylvania vs. Larry Stromberg. Petition for Allowance of Appeal. April 19, 1999, I.D. No. 22731; p. 30.

Chapter 2:

    1. In the Court of Common Pleas of Philadelphia County. First Judicial District of Pennsylvania. Criminal Trial Division. Commonwealth of Pennsylvania v. Larry Stromberg. March 16, 1998; N.T. 5/30/97, pp. 98-99; N.T. 5/8/97, pp. 101-102; N.T. 5/30/97, pp. 159-160, 163; N.T. 5/29/97, pp. 157-158; N.T. 6/3/97, pp. 40, 122; N.T. 5/29/97, pp. 54, 58; N.T. 5/29/97, pp. 61-63; N.T. 5/28/97, p. 134; N.T. 5/28/97, pp. 128-130, 132-133, 139-141; N.T. 6/2/97, pp. 17-84, 119-124, 131-154, 180-186; N.T. 6/3/97, pp. 38-40, 106-113, 122-127.

    2. IBID. N.T. 5/28/97, p. 135; N.T. 5/28/97, p. 136; N.T. 5/28/97, p. 135; N.T. 5/30/97, pp. 25-26; N.T. 5/30/97, p. 27.

    3. IBID. N.T. 5/29/97, pp.150-153.

    4. IBID. N.T. 5/28/97, pp. 72-77.

    5. IBID. N.T. 5/28/97, p. 100; N.T. 4/28/96, p. 100; N.T. 4/28/96, p. 101; N.T. 4/28/96, p. 101.

    6. IBID. N.T. 5/28/97, pp. 118-125; N.T. 5/28/97, p. 128; N.T. 5/28/97, p. 135; N.T. 5/28/97, pp.135-136; N.T. 5/28/97, p.136; N.T. 5/28/97, p. 28; N.T. 5/29/97, p. 136; N.T. 5/28/97, p. 153; N.T. 5/28/97, pp. 156-157.

7. IBID. N.T. 5/29/97, pp. 43-45; N.T. 5/29/97, pp. 54-58; N.T. 5/29/97, p. 63; N.T. 5/29/97, p. 65; N.T. 5/29/97, pp. 65-75; N.T. 5/29/97, p. 84.
8. IBID. N.T. 5/29/97, p. 152.
9. IBID. N.T. 5/29/97, p. 157; N.T. 5/29/97, p. 164.
10. IBID. N.T. 5/29/97, pp. 170-180.
11. IBID. N.T. 5/29/97, pp. 196-201.
12. IBID. N.T. 5/29/97, pp. 196-201.
13. IBID. N.T. 5/29/97, p. 213.
14. IBID. N.T. 5/30/97, pp. 21-24.
15. IBID. N.T. 5/30/97, pp. 31-35.
16. IBID. N.T. 5/30/97, p. 39; N.T. 5/30/97, pp. 38-39; N.T. 5/30/97, pp. 40-41.
17. IBID. N.T. 5/30/97, p. 66; N.T. 5/30/97, p. 75.
18. IBID. N.T. 5/30/97, pp. 83-84; N.T. 5/30/97, pp. 84-85; N.T. 5/30/97, p.86; N.T. 5/30/97, pp.89-103; N.T. 5/30/97, p. 113.
19. IBID. N.T. 6/2/97, p. 12.
20. IBID. N.T. 5/30/97, p. 185.

Chapter 3:
1. In the Court of Common Pleas of Philadelphia County. First Judicial District of Pennsylvania. Criminal Trial Division. Commonwealth of Pennsylvania v. Larry Stromberg. March 16, 1998; N.T. 6/2/97, p. 30; N.T. 6/2/97, p. 49; N.T. 6/2/97, p. 50; N.T. 6/2/97, p. 74.
2. IBID. N.T. 6/3/97, pp. 11-20; N.T. 6/3/97, pp. 22-23.
3. IBID. N.T. 6/3/97, pp. 36-37; N.T. 6/3/97, pp. 40-46; N.T. 6/3/97, pp.51-53; N.T. 6/3/97, p. 83.
4. IBID. N.T. 6/3/97, pp. 129-130; N.T. 6/3/97, p. 134; N.T. 6/3/97, p. 137; N.T. 6/3/97, p. 136.
5. IBID. N.T. 6/3/97, p. 215; N.T. 6/4/97, pp. 10-12; N.T. 6/3/97, p. 219; N.T. 6/4/97, p. 220; N.T. 6/4/97, pp. 18-19.

6. IBID. N.T. 6/4/97, p. 133; N.T. 6/4/97, pp. 129-130; N.T. 6/4/97, pp. 130-131; N.T. 6/4/97, p. 136; N.T. 6/4/97, pp.152-158; N.T. 6/4/97, pp. 160-166; N.T. 6/4/97, p. 167; N.T. 6/4/97, p. 193; N.T. 6/4/97, pp. 170-171.

7. IBID. N.T. 6/4/97, pp. 245-246.

8. IBID. N.T. 6/5/97, p. 80; N.T. 6/5/97, p. 87; N.T. 6/5/97, pp. 97-98, 101, 107, 115, 117; N.T. 6/5/97, p. 121; N.T. 6/5/97, p. 132; N.T. 6/5/97, p. 136.

9. IBID. N.T. 6/9/97.

Chapter 5:

1. McNaghten Rules, Wikipedia.com; findlaw.com from Merriam-Webster's Dictionary of Law c1996 Merriam-Webster, Incorporated. "The Insanity Defense Among the States – http://criminal.findlaw.com/criminal-procedure/the-insanity-defense-among-the-states.html.

2. IBID.

3. IBID.

4. IBID.

5. In the Court of Common Pleas of Philadelphia County. First Judicial District of Pennsylvania. Criminal Trial Division. Commonwealth of Pennsylvania v. Larry Stromberg. March 16, 1998; N.T. 5/30/97, p. 185.

6. Rendine, Daniel A.; Petition for Allowance of Appeal, Commonwealth of Pennsylvania vs. Larry Stromberg; In the Supreme Court of Pennsylvania, Philadelphia District April 19, 1999, I.D. No. 22731; p. i.

Acting, Directing, Producing, Screenwriting Career

Appendix A

Film & Television performances 1986-96 & 2016:

Date:	Title:	Role:
1986	*George Washington: A Forging of a Nation*	extra
	Seasons in the Sun	best friend
	[student film for Temple University]	
	The Beat [NYC student]	extra
1987	*Gruesome's Legend* [lead role]	Tony
	[written & produced by L.N. Stromberg]	
	Homeless [NYC]	extra
	Blades [on HBO]	Don
	Clean and Sober	extra
	Flying Blind	extra
1988	*Penn and Teller Get Killed*	extra
	Glitz	extra
	The Lemon Sisters	extra
1989	*Shannon's Deal*	extra
1990	*Life with Mikey*	extra
	Rocky V	extra
	Annabelle	boyfriend
	[student film for Temple University]	
1991	*Malcom X*	extra
	Mannequin Two: On the Move	mid-level soldier
	Ventman	thug
	[student film for NY School of Visual Arts]	
	I Don't Buy Kisses Anymore	silent bit
	[at bus station with Jason Alexander & Nia Peeples]	
1992	*Philadelphia*	extra

	[starring Tom Hanks & Denzel Washington]	
	Horrorscope	Eddie
	[written, directed & produced by L.N. Stromberg]	
1993	*Heavenbound*	Mac
	[written, directed & produced by L.N. Stromberg]	
	Money for Nothing	dockworker
	[at docks with John Cusack, Philip Seymour Hoffman & James Gandolfini]	
	Two Bits	extra
1994	*Master Race from Mars*	sailor
	Moving	mover
	[Temple University student film]	
	Flicker in the Dark	thug
	Rats in the Maze	robber
1995	*IQ*	extra
	[starring Tim Robbins, Meg Ryan & Walter Matthau]	
	Up Close and Personal	extra
	[starring Robert Redford & Michelle Pfeiffer]	
	Records	extra
1996	*Wide Awake*	extra
	Maximum Risk	extra
	The Father, the Son	hitman
	Life at the End of Time	loud-mouth customer
	12 Monkeys	extra
	[starring Bruce Willis, Madeleine Stowe & Brad Pitt]	
	Terrorism	extra
2016	*Spiritual Warfare*	lead role
	[written, produced & directed by L.N. Stromberg]	

Appendix B

Screenplays written by Larry Stromberg:

Gruesome's Legend

Spiritual Warfare

Spiritual Warfare – The War Continues

Spiritual Warfare 2

Spiritual Warfare 3

Spiritual Warfare 4

Theater of the Dead

Father Shaw

The Gift of Love

Eastern State

The Penitentiary

A Meeting with the Offender

The Appalachian Beast

The Steroid Connection

Horrorscope

Heavenbound

Appendix C

Stage performances 1973-96:

Year:	Title:		Role:
1973	*Santa Claus is Coming to Town*		Santa
	[elementary school play]		
1982	*South Pacific*		sailor
1986	*The Wrong Bank*		Leo
	[at Lansdowne Theater written & directed by L.N. Stromberg]		
	Charlie and Algernon	[Stra-bis-Mus Theater]	Frank
1988	*You Gotta be Saved*		Roy
	[church play]		
	Celebrate Life		John the Baptist
	[church play]		
	Richard the III		first murderer
	[Colonial Playhouse]		
	Dial M for Murder		Capt. Lesgate Swann
	[Footlighters Theater]		
1989	*Harvey*		orderly
	[Colonial Playhouse]		
	Death of a Salesman		Happy Loman
	[Footlighters Theater]		
	Arsenic and Old Lace		Jonathan Brewster
	[Footlighters Theater]		
1990	*Our Town*		George Gibbs
	[Germantown Players]		
1991	*A Change is Gonna Come*		Troy
	[The Actors Center-Philadelphia]		
1995-96	*Tony and Tina's Wedding*		Dominick Fabrizzi
	[South Philly Theater Interaction Productions]		

Stromberg also acted in numerous commercials, music videos and training films in the Philadelphia, Delaware and New Jersey areas.

Appendix D

All plays listed were written, directed & produced by L.N. Stromberg unless otherwise noted.

Stage productions at S.C.I. Coal Township:

Year:	Title:	Role:
1999	*True Meaning of Christmas*	Tony
2000	*The Persecution on Christmas Eve*	Dom
2002	*No Greater Love*	Joey
	Holy Night	Lou
2003	*Good Brothers 1*	Frank
	Good Brothers 2	Frank
	Mother's Day	best friend
	Father's Day	best friend
	A Christmas of Trust	John
2004	*The Forgiven*	Lenny Stone
2006	*Crossroads*	Bruno
	The Sojourner	Calvin
2007	*The Bible Study*	Mike
	Trinity	rap singer
	The Prince of Peace	man about to commit suicide
2008	*Heavenbound*	Mac Stone
	Spiritual Warfare	the devil
	The Gift of Love	Jay
	Dr. Elf and Santa the Man	Dr. Elf
2009	*The Pretender*	crazy man
	Mother's Day 2	best friend
	Don't Look Back [short play]	
	Lively Hope [short play]	
	By Grace	Tommy
	Christmas Memories	lone man

	Spiritual Intimidations	thug
2010	*Two Christians, Who are You?*	Pastor
	Hall of Faith	
	The Marathon	runner
	The Mercy Seat	Mike
2011	*The Resurrection and the Life*	thief at the cross
	Warware	Michael
	Christmas Honor	veteran
2012	*I, Paul*	King Nero
	The Visit	Pastor
2013	*A Brother's Love*	cellmate
	Judgement	voice of God
2014	*The Professor and the Student*	professor

At S.C.I. Graterford:

Year:	**Title:**	**Role:**
2015	*Anistemi* [written with Jermaine Weeks]	drunk
	Coming Home	parole agent Mark
	[written and directed by Jermaine Weeks]	
	A Meeting with the Offender	Romero
	Fight Another Day [performed at the Philadelphia Fight Center by former inmates; directed by Professor David Ingram & Celeste Walker, produced by Alma Sanchez-Eppler/Philadelphia Fights Institute for Community Justice]	
	Up from the Depths	narrator
	Fight Another Day	Leo
	[performed at S.C.I. Graterford]	
	Christmas Memories	
	Santa and the Two Elves	
2016	*I Plead the Blood!*	Satan
	[written with Jermaine Weeks]	

Life Behind the Razor Wire   Franco

Many of Stromberg's plays are available for reading at www.prisonsfoundation.org.

The following plays haven't yet been staged:
> *Voice of the Victim*
> *I'm Sorry*
> *Letters to the Victims*
> *Criminally Insane*
> *The Chair, the Suffering of Janet*

Appendix E

Other Activities & Programs

1999-2015 Choir (at S.C.I Coal Township):
Member of the Church Christian

1999-present (at S.C.I. Coal Township & S.C.I. Graterford):
Pennsylvania Runathon – alternatives to incarceration of youth (4 years)
Certificate of Baptism
Environmental Concepts
Life Losses – Psychology Department
Free as an Eagle course
Peer Education Program
Certificate of Completion typing program
Cornerstone prison ministry discipleship program
Intramural powerlifting (4 years)
Triumph certificate
Blood and body spill fluid spill clean-up program (5 years)
Second Chance Ministries International, Inc. "Walking your Faith" program
The Bethesda Family Services Foundation – "Learn and Live" – a life skills program
Lifers Incorporated at Graterford – certificate of recognition
Day of Responsibility – The Pennsylvania Prison Society
Violence Prevention Moderate Intensity Program completed
Celebrate Recovery Program – current
Temple University Department of Criminal Justice program – "Inside/Out" – current
Villanova Criminal Justice Program – current

Jobs at S.C.I Coal Township & Graterford
Coal Township:

       Block-worker – 4 years

       Educational janitor (school building) – 4 years

       Medical janitor (in medical department) – 5 years

       Gym/Activities worker – 4 years

Graterford:

       Staff dining hall

About the Author

MJ Maccalupo is the author of four other books, which includes three novels: *Where the Road Begins, Murder at Ravenswood Hall* and *The Allentown Murders*, and one collection, *The Almost Definitive Collection, vol. 1.*

He has also written a non-fiction book on leadership, *Leadership: IQ vs. EQ*, and a journal-writing program for students in elementary, middle and high school called, *Journaling with Character.*

All his books can be purchased from your local bookstore, on line, as well as from his website at www.mjmaccalupo.com. They are available in paperback as well as eBooks.

He has been a guest on several radio and morning television programs in Buffalo, NY, and Wilmington and Raleigh, NC including: (television) *Winging It! Buffalo Style* with Victoria Hong, Allie Hartwick, Joe Arena and Lauren Hall; *A.M. Buffalo* with Linda Pellegrino, and (radio) *WNED* with Mike Desmond in Buffalo, NY, *WHQR* with Jemila Ericson in Wilmington, NC, and *WPTF* with Brian Freeman in Raleigh, NC.

His books have been reviewed in *Encore Magazine*, *The Wilmington Star News* and *The Buffalo News*.

He lives along the Southeastern North Carolina Coast with his wife and two dogs.

Made in the USA
Columbia, SC
02 July 2017